FUGITIVES

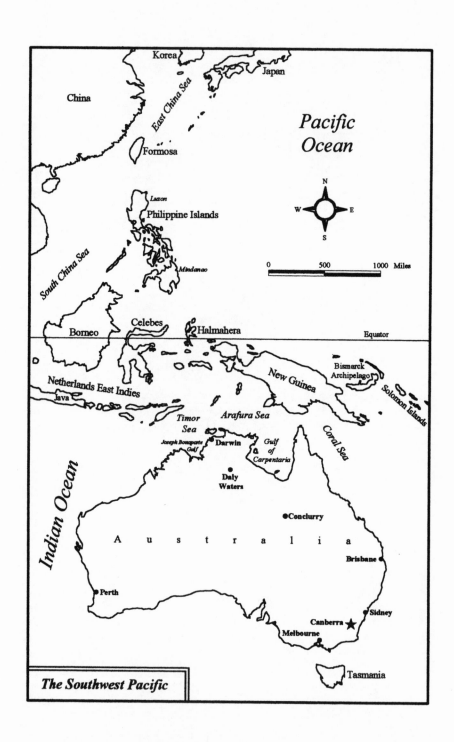

Korea

Japan

China

East China Sea

Formosa

Pacific Ocean

N
W   E
S

Luzon
Philippine Islands

South China Sea

Mindanao

0   500   1000   Miles

Borneo

Celebes

Halmahera

Equator

Bismarck Archipelago

New Guinea

Solomon Islands

Netherlands East Indies

Java

Timor Sea

Arafura Sea

Coral Sea

Joseph Bonaparte Gulf

Darwin

Gulf of Carpentaria

Daly Waters

Indian Ocean

A   u   s   t   r   a   l   i   a

●Cloncurry

Brisbane ●

Perth ●

Sidney ●

Canberra ★

Melbourne ●

Tasmania

The Southwest Pacific

FUGITIVES

EVADING AND ESCAPING THE JAPANESE

bob stahl

THE UNIVERSITY PRESS OF KENTUCKY

Published by The University Press of Kentucky,
scholarly publisher for the Commonwealth,
serving Bellarmine University, Berea College,
Centre College of Kentucky, Eastern Kentucky University,
The Filson Historical Society, Georgetown College,
Kentucky Historical Society, Kentucky State University,
Morehead State University, Murray State University,
Northern Kentucky University, Transylvania University,
University of Kentucky, University of Louisville,
and Western Kentucky University.

Editorial and Sales Offices: The University Press of Kentucky
663 South Limestone Street, Lexington, Kentucky 40508-4008

01 02 03 04 05   5 4 3 2 1

Library of Congress Cataloging-in-Publication Data

Stahl, Bob, 1920-
Fugitives : evading and escaping the Japanese / Bob Stahl.
p. cm.
ISBN 0-8131-2224-4 (alk. paper)
1. World War, 1939-1945—Philippines—Fiction. 2. Mining
engineers—Fiction. 3. Pacific Ocean—Fiction. 4. Sailing—
Fiction. I. Title.
PS3619.T47 F84 2001
813'.54—dc21   2001004663

This book is printed on acid-free recycled paper meeting
the requirements of the American National Standard
for Permanence in Paper for Printed Library Materials.

Manufactured in the United States of America.

CONTENTS

MAPS

PREFACE

Little recorded in history are the events in the lives of the expatriates, mostly American, employed by the various industries and the government in the Philippine Islands. Doctors, nurses, educators, accountants, engineers, lumbermen, agriculturalists, governmental administrators, and a host of other specialists have been drawn to the Philippines ever since the Spanish-American War. With the start of the hostilities of World War II these men, women, and their families suddenly found themselves trapped behind enemy lines facing a series of crises never remotely anticipated. They were suddenly forced to relocate from the population centers to the rural areas or to the mountainous jungle and fend for themselves in an unknown—perhaps even hostile—environment. One such individual was Jordan A. Hamner.

"Ham" Hamner had entered Oregon State University in 1920 at the age of sixteen. For ten years he alternated periods of work with periods of study in pursuit of a degree in mining engineering, graduating just in time to become one more victim of the bleak economy of the Great Depression.

For the next three years Hamner found jobs in mines which soon after closed because of the economic conditions of the period. Finally, in California, he found a mine with sufficient financial stability to survive despite the surrounding economic chaos. There Hamner eked out a livelihood for himself, his wife, Dorothy, whom he married in 1933, and his son, Rick, born in 1937.

In 1941, a much better job opportunity came to him provided that he relocate his family overseas to the Philippine Islands. He saw this as a way to escape the hand-to-mouth existence he and his family were enduring and accepted the position. Again Fate dealt him a bad hand. Before he was able to have his family join him overseas, he became the victim of a condition far, far worse than an economic

Jordan Hamner. (Courtesy of Rick Hamner)

Jordan and Dorothy Hamner after his return from the war. (Courtesy of Rick Hamner)

depression. Hamner was forced into an active role as a participant in World War II.

Twenty-seven years after the end of World War II, Jordan Hamner set to paper memories of his hide-and-seek existence behind the Japanese lines. To insure the accuracy of his story, he revisited the islands of the South Pacific, recalling the fears, frustrations, anxieties, pains, pleasures—all the emotions he had experienced during a year of fugitive wandering in a hostile land. The result was a detailed account of the escapades he and his friends survived while successfully eluding the Japanese.

In December 1943, I became a member of an Allied Intelligence Bureau (AIB) penetration party to Samar Island led by Maj. Charles M. Smith. Our mission was to establish a network of clandestine radio stations overlooking the sea lanes in the area and to report Japanese shipping movements to U.S. Naval Intelligence. We were also called upon to collect and relay to the AIB headquarters in Australia any intelligence information we could gather from the Manila area and southern Luzon, Leyte, and Samar. On many lonesome evenings in the jungle, Major Smith, who had been one of Hamner's partners on the *Or Else* voyage, broke the monotony by relating bits of the story of their adventures. Although many years have passed, the details of Smith's stories have stuck in my memory and are amazingly consistent with those in Hamner's memoir. Occasionally I have drawn on my own wartime experiences in the Philippines or enhanced Hamner's observations with details provided by Smith. These additions comprise a very small portion of the entire work and have been made silently. What readers will find herein is a true historical adventure story based on the memoir of Jordan A. Hamner.

Without Hamner's memoir, this story would have gone to the grave with him, and another of the many extremely important but unrecorded parts of the history of World War II would have been lost forever. Nor could this book have been written and published without the generous cooperation of Rick Hamner, who granted permission to use his father's memoir as a basis for this work. To the Hamners, father and son, I am most deeply indebted.

Along the way, many others have had a hand in helping the work come to life: Douglas Clanin, an editor for the Indiana Historical

Society who, through interviews with a host of survivors of the Bataan Death March, of guerrillas who resisted the Japanese during the enemy's occupation of the islands and of participants in the successful recapture of the islands, has gained a formidable knowledge of this vital part of history, critiqued early copies of the manuscript; Andrew Pearson, an independent producer of television programs, who also critiqued early copies of the manuscript; Peter Parsons, a writer, who contributed continuous review of my writings along with much encouragement; and Jaime Alvarez, a cartographer, who prepared the detailed maps.

Members of the American Guerrillas of Mindanao who knew and remembered Hamner provided background information about locales and events they shared in the dark days of 1942. James Zobel, curator of the MacArthur Museum, Norfolk, Virginia, proved to be most helpful in many ways, as was Dr. Richard Sommers, archivist-historian of the U.S. Army Military History Institute, Carlisle, Pennsylvania. Many others have lent much appreciated encouragement when it was desperately needed. Primary in that group is my wife, Ruth, who put up with my dour moods and would not let me quit when the going got tough. Thank you all.

INTRODUCTION

On the morning of 7 December 1941, the Japanese attacked the United States military and naval forces in the Hawaiian Islands, leaving them in complete disarray. A few hours later, across the international date line in the Philippine Islands, they destroyed the U.S. Army Air Corps at Clark Field, Luzon, on 8 December. Their devastating attacks on Cavite Naval Yard and the Manila harbor within the next few days decimated the few vessels constituting the navy's Asiatic Fleet.

In 1935, Gen. Douglas A. MacArthur was sent to the Philippines to establish a military training and defense program. He retired in 1939, but returned to duty in July 1941 to command the United States Forces in the Far East (USAFFE), a combination of American and Philippine ground troops. This force was inadequately manned, equipped, and trained to defend the islands against the powerful Japanese onslaught. With his troops falling back toward Manila from every front, General MacArthur declared the capital an open city on 25 December 1941 to prevent its destruction by Japanese air and artillery bombardments, a declaration ignored completely by the Japanese as they continued to shell the city mercilessly. The defenders were withdrawn to Bataan Peninsula and to Corregidor Island to provide a delaying action while awaiting reinforcement. The expected assisting troops, aircraft, and supplies never arrived, for Congress and President Franklin Delano Roosevelt had declared war not just on the Japanese but upon the Axis coalition—Germany, Italy, and Japan. With his nation incapable of conducting a major war on two fronts, President Roosevelt chose to make the war in Europe his primary concern and sent all available troops and materiel to that theater, leaving the USAFFE without support.

General MacArthur established a headquarters on Corregidor Island, the bastion where he would make a last-ditch stand, if necessary. But President Roosevelt ordered him to Australia to regroup the Allied military forces, and he left Corregidor 11 March 1942. Gen. Jonathan M. Wainwright assumed command and continued to lead a valiant but hopeless fight against the Japanese. The overwhelmed troops on Bataan were already in complete disarray, victims of starvation, sickness, and an almost total lack of medical supplies and facilities to treat the wounded. On 9 April, Bataan was surrendered. Seventy-eight thousand American and Filipino troops were taken prisoner and force-marched under most inhuman treatment in the infamous Bataan Death March to filthy, overcrowded prisons, where more than ten thousand died. Some managed to escape during the march or from the prisons and made their way into the mountainous jungle, only to die of starvation or illness unless they were fortunate enough to be rescued and cared for by natives.

Corregidor now fell under siege and was overwhelmed by the Japanese assault in less than a month. On 6 May 1942, General Wainwright surrendered Corregidor and its 11,500 troops. He was taken prisoner, not to be released until 1945. His troops were moved to the Luzon mainland then marched to prison in a manner not unlike that of the Bataan Death March. The rest of Luzon and the other islands fell like dominoes.

The Japanese soon established a puppet government under Jose P. Laurel in place of the elected government led by President Manuel L. Quezon, who, with several other high government officials, moved to America. The Japanese arrested and interrogated other governmental officials and businessmen, many of whom were imprisoned, some executed, for posing a possible danger to the incoming government. The Japanese also mistreated the U.S. Army and Navy nurses, American citizens, and expatriates from other Allied countries, most of whom were crowded into Santo Tomas University in Manila under intolerable living conditions and there subjected to inhuman treatment throughout the war.

Although the primary arena for combat between the Japanese and the Allied troops was on Luzon, the repercussions of the Japanese victory were felt by some fifteen million Filipino civilians scattered over the archipelago's four hundred populated islands. News of the Japanese atrocities on Luzon quickly spread to the other islands. When the Japanese occupation forces that replaced the combat troops gradually spread throughout the islands to the populated areas, they resorted to the same pattern of cruel and inhumane punishment for the slightest infraction of the arbitrary rules they imposed upon the Filipinos. Those who openly resisted the Japanese were tortured and executed before forced assemblages of townspeople.

Many Filipino families deserted the towns and moved into the jungle. There men organized into small bands to protect their jungle homes and families against Japanese patrols. These bands became larger and stronger with the addition of American military personnel who had not surrendered to the Japanese or who had escaped from Japanese prison camps. The Americans needed food and shelter and traded their military skills for these commodities. Out of these unions came skilled guerrilla teams that soon joined with other teams to carry out a high level of anti-Japanese guerrilla warfare. The size of the guerrilla armies varied from island to island, the largest being on Mindanao where it numbered close to thirty-five thousand men when the United States returned to the islands in 1945. These troops were instrumental in the retaking of the islands.

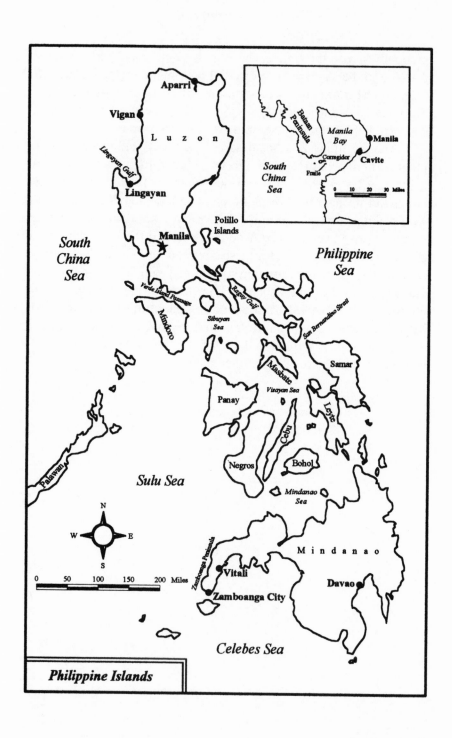

PROLOGUE

That night we were hit by a series of squalls that came from nowhere. We dropped the sail and rolled free on large waves. Charlie Smith and Catalina took shelter from the rain below deck in the tiny cabin. Chick, Lakibul, and I huddled under ponchos on deck, with Lakibul at the tiller. An especially strong squall hit us and the boat tipped over. The mast was flat out on the water. Chick, Lakibul, and I were spilled overboard, along with many of the supplies stored on deck. We clung to the high side of the boat, and as we clambered to get up out of the water, the boat righted itself. She was full of water, but stayed afloat. We bailed like mad for about an hour, using any container we could find that would hold water. We were cold, miserable, and scared.

The boat was finally emptied. The squalls departed, but not without taking a heavy toll. All of our water had been spilled. All of our rice, which we had been carefully rationing, had gotten wet. All of our sugar was wet. Save for a few floating coconuts that we were able to fish out of the sea, we were without water and had a minuscule amount of food. On the bright side, we still had a sail—and fuel for the engine. And best of all, we were still alive.

Soon after daybreak on a morning in August 1941, the S.S. *Annie Johnson* hove-to in the center of North Channel, the narrower of the two inlets to Manila Bay. There, along with several other vessels, she sat motionlessly, her propellers turning ever so slowly to hold her steady against the tide while her rudder headed her bow into a light northeast wind. The vessels were awaiting an escort to guide them to the Manila harbor.

A mile to starboard stood Corregidor Island; the same distance to port stood the southern tip of Bataan Peninsula—two obscure geographic points destined soon to take places in history beside Valley Forge and the Alamo. Dead ahead a maze of mines floated just below the surface, each tethered by a steel cable to an anchor on the ocean's floor, barring the *Annie Johnson's* entrance to Manila Bay and the docks of the city of Manila—*The Pearl of the Orient*—the capital of the Philippines.

Corregidor Island. Three miles long but with a width best measured in yards, the island resembled a grotesque, overgrown tadpole. Facing the South China Sea, its volcanic rock head—Topside—rose to more than six hundred feet above the beach. Trailing to the east, its body lay closer to sea level except for one small bulge—Malinta Hill. Ill concealed on Topside were some of the largest and most accurate coast artillery pieces possessed by the United States Army. Well concealed in Malinta Hill was a honeycomb of tunnels containing a command post, barracks, mess hall, infirmary, munitions dump, motor pool—all the services that normally are housed in buildings at a military fortress. East of Malinta Hill was a small airport—Kindley Field.

Bataan Peninsula. A background of soft light-green forest framed the bamboo and nipa huts lining its shore. Dugouts and small sailboats, some with one outrigger and others with two, moved close along the coast. Hidden in this idyllic setting were more coast artillery pieces poised to join with Topside in unleashing on any invading naval force a fury seldom, if ever, before seen in warfare on the sea.

The North Channel was the only route open from the South China Sea to the bay, for the eight-mile-wide South Channel was mined so heavily that one foolish enough to try it might find it possible to cross from the shore of Corregidor to Fraile Island and from thence to Cavite Province by stepping from one lethal floating device to the next.

Prologue 3

The Manila Bay entrance—built, rebuilt, and expanded since the 1900s—was the Gibraltar of the Orient, a bastion which would keep Manila safe from intrusion by any enemy. Or so it was thought.

one

MANILA

Magnuson described the Army Day parade held in Manila earlier in the year. "Hundreds of tanks, armored cars, artillery pieces, and all kinds of military gear rolled along the parade route, while air corps fighters and bombers zoomed overhead. It was an awesome display of power."

Although the trip from Los Angeles to Manila on the S.S. *Annie Johnson* was uneventful, I did not look upon it as a relaxing ocean cruise. Good food, swimming in a twenty-foot-square canvas pool on the afterdeck, lying on a deck chair while sipping drinks which got more and more tropical as we moved closer and closer to the equator kept me occupied. But the news broadcasts describing the diplomatic confrontations between the United States and Japan were of more than casual concern to me and to many other passengers, although we seldom spoke of them. War with the Japanese was a possibility no one wanted to admit even to himself, so everyone avoided the subject in conversations while individually speculating on the future and hoping for the best.

I met Harry Magnuson, personnel manager for a stevedoring company in Manila, as we were boarding ship in San Francisco. An American, Harry had resided in the Philippines for ten years and was returning to Luzon after a short business trip to California. Recognizing that I was new to ocean liner travel, he volunteered some tips on shipboard procedures that simplified my getting settled aboard. On the second day out we met again when I spotted him reclining on a canvas lounger in the shade of one of the upper decks. I sat next to him and from then on, as if by prearrangement, we met at the same spot to chat each morning.

Harry gave me an excellent briefing on life in the Philippines— the relationship between Americans and Filipinos, the business climate, the culture. And, apart from the other passengers, we shared our ideas about the possibility of a confrontation with the Japanese.

Magnuson described the Army Day parade held in Manila earlier in the year. "Hundreds of tanks, armored cars, artillery pieces, and all kinds of military gear rolled along the parade route, while air corps fighters and bombers zoomed overhead. It was an awesome display of power. The Japanese wouldn't have a chance if they tried to take these islands," he said.

"And we've got the biggest and most powerful navy in the world," I volunteered. "We'd blast the Jap fleet out of the water and cut their supply lines even if their army was, somehow, able to make a landing here."

"You're right about that. And if we can't, we'll call on the Britishers to help."

No, we wouldn't be too bad off if war came. It would be a short and minor conflict. Yet our doubts put a damper on much of the trip.

After spending the decade of the 20s alternating periods of work with periods of study, I obtained a degree in mining engineering just as the world was entering the Great Depression. I worked at several mines that soon closed because of the sluggish economic conditions before finding one with a modicum of financial stability. Now, at the age of thirty-six, I was making a career move that would take me, my wife, Dot, and our four-year-old son, Rick, away from the life on the fringe of poverty we had been enduring. I had accepted a position as a mine foreman at the Masbate Consolidated Gold Mines on the central Philippine Island that bears the same name, Masbate.

My traveling alone to the Philippine Islands was not intentional. I had little difficulty obtaining a passport for myself, but a family passport was unavailable at the time. Dot and Rick would have to follow me to this tropical paradise later, I was told, with only a vague explanation as to why. The unrevealed reason: the State Department was trying to get Americans and their families *out* of the Orient and the Pacific islands. War against the Japanese was an accepted certainty our country's leaders were concealing from the people. It was only a matter of time. In fact, war was imminent.

Passports for my wife and son were never issued. Our plans for a new start in the Philippines did not materialize. Our lives did not turn out quite as we had planned.

Finally underway after several hours of waiting, our convoy, consisting of the *Annie Johnson*, the S.S. *Corregidor*, and several smaller ships, carefully sailed a zig-zag course through the minefield, escorted by a gleaming white yacht flying both the American and Philippine flags. Slowly, we proceeded toward Manila, some twenty-five miles away. Soon the impatient *Corregidor* sped past us and was out of sight before the skyline of Manila was visible. The captain of that fast inter-island passenger ship had made this convoy run many times before, and after passing a certain point, he left the convoy to thread his path through the rest of the minefield alone. Four months later, the *Corregidor* would be a victim of this minefield, with a very heavy loss of life, when she struck a mine that was floating free after breaking loose from its mooring.

The Manila skyline was far different from what I'd expected. Large concrete and marble buildings with an American look loomed high on the horizon, the background for a conglomeration of old and new storage buildings and decrepit hovels along the shore. As our ship passed port side to the waterfront, the hovels were revealed to be bamboo-framed shacks wrapped and roofed with tinder-dry brown nipa palm fronds. Intermingled with the bamboo shacks were galvanized iron *bodegas*, or warehouses. In sharp contrast, the elegant Manila Hotel with its nine-hole golf course and swimming pools appeared directly ahead.

A half-mile from shore, a low rock breakwater protected the port from the heavy seas that accompany tropical storms, with narrow entrances leading into the inner harbor. Just outside this barrier, the *Annie Johnson* stopped as an inspection launch tied up alongside. First aboard was a United States Government health officer whose inspection was unexpectedly brief, for he was interested only in smallpox vaccination certificates. The Philippine immigration inspectors who followed him subjected us to a more meticulous examination. About fifteen of them took two hours to check our passports before our ship moved through the breakwater and tied up at Pier Seven, which was, I was reminded periodically for the next three years, the largest pier in the world. It could very well have owned that distinction, for ours was one of three transpacific ships tied up bow to stern, with dock space to spare. There, the customs inspectors boarded and checked us for contraband and firearms. We finally were permitted to move down the gangplank, and once on the dock, I hired a *calesa*, a horse-drawn cart, to carry me and my baggage to one of the finest hotels in the Orient.

The Manila Hotel sported a new, fancy, air-conditioned section that had recently been added to the quaint, old, utile building on which the hotel's reputation had been earned. I was given space in the quaint part, which was indeed fancy but far from air-conditioned and very different. Very, very different.

My room was large, about twenty feet square, with an adjacent small bathroom area fitted with ceramic tile floor and walls and modern fixtures. The bedroom's twelve-foot-high ceiling was probably intended to give the hot, humid air plenty of room to rise. It didn't all get to the top. The transition from extremely hot to bearably hot occurred at head-height when I extended my six-foot frame erect. The temperature was much more bearable when I was seated. The doorway to the hall was six feet wide and eight feet high, with double doors fitted with immovable louvers. Above the doorway, extending the entire width of the room and reaching to the ceiling, was open latticework that added to the circulation of air as well as any noises. Soundproof the room was not.

The window in the opposite wall, about six feet wide and five feet high, without glass but with sliding shutters made of four-inch squares of a seashell-like material, afforded a great view of the golf course and the city beyond. Below the window stool and dropping to the floor was another opening with iron grills and sliding doors. Outside the window was a five-foot eave from which a green bamboo rolling curtain could be lowered or raised by ropes and pulleys to shield out the sun.

The rest of the walls and the ceiling were covered with tan abaca cloth, quite attractive except for some seams where the paste had failed and the edges of the cloth had peeled a bit, creating a discontinuous, shadowy, irregular stripe. Randomly spaced around the room were ancient gas sconces that had been wired to provide electric lighting.

Suspended from the ceiling near the center of the room by two-foot-long ropes at each end was a four-foot-long bamboo pole. Attached to the pole were several wide palm fronds. A rope draped loosely from the center of the pole to a hook at head-height on the wall. I envisioned in days long past a servant squatting on the floor beneath this hook with rope in hand swinging the fan from side to side to stir the air while his master and mistress slept in one or both of the double beds. The beds were surrounded by mosquito nets that were rolled up during the day and dropped at night.

The bed, dresser, and armoire were made of black mahogany that bore in relief hand-carved designs depicting palm trees, sailing canoes, and pineapples. The rest of the furnishings—a nightstand and two chairs—were wicker creations. Finishing off the decor was a highly polished mahogany floor covered sporadically with buri palm rugs.

The Manila Hotel compared favorably with the best American hotels of the period. It had a large lobby, comfortably furnished with overstuffed chairs and sofas, a fine restaurant, attractive bars and taprooms, a nightclub, shops, and hundreds of bellboys—each one with his hand out, just like in the States.

My stateside wool suit was more than a little uncomfortable in this climate, so I shed my jacket and tie, rolled up my shirt sleeves, and set out to find a tailor. The street outside the main entrance to the hotel was alive with vendors hawking all manner of goods and foods. I spotted a man with a pushcart peddling a variety of tropical fruits. He wore a short-sleeved cotton shirt and shorts, both a faded blue with the edges tattered from many washes. His feet shuffled along the sidewalk in wood-soled sandals. A red bandana protected his head from the sun. Most of his fruits I did not recognize, so I selected several bananas, although they were of a rosy color rather than the yellow I was used to.

"Don't you have any yellow bananas?"

"Oh, no, Sair! These are 'Baguio bananas.' Much sweeter! Much better, Sair."

"How much?" It was then that I realized that I had no Philippine currency. I hadn't yet exchanged any dollars for pesos.

"They are two centavos each, Sair. You have five, Sair. That is ten centavos, Sair."

I knew that the exchange rate was two pesos for one dollar— two centavos for a penny. I reached into my pocket for some change, selected a nickel and offered it to the Filipino.

"But, Sair," said the vendor, "do you not have any centavos?"

"No. All I have is American money. Isn't this enough?"

"Oh, but Sair. If you do not have centavos, Sair, I must charge you the same amount in cents, Sair. It is the law, Sair."

I recognized that I was being conned, but gave the vendor another nickel. After all, a nickel wasn't a bad fee for getting a valuable lesson. I had learned that the Filipinos were pretty sharp, and that I should be careful in dealing with them. And I noted that the bigger the con the more often the word "Sair" entered into the conversation.

"Is there a tailor shop nearby?" I asked the vendor.

"Oh, yes Sair. For ten centavos—I mean ten cents, Sair—I will show the way, Sair."

"Okay," I said, and handed him a dime.

He pushed his cart about fifty feet from where we were standing and stopped.

"In there, Sair," he said, pointing to a door labeled:

LO CHIN
CUSTOM TAILOR
UPSTAIRS

I had been taken again.

Lo Chin could have been named "No Chin," for what God intended to be his chin blended into the blubber on his chest without a break. Three hundred pounds of man squatted on the floor amidst a legless sewing machine, a basket of threads, needles, and pins, and many bolts of cloth—and he wore a broad smile under twinkling eyes. Wrapped in a beautifully embroidered silk robe, he looked like the reincarnation of Buddha. It was obvious that his worktable was the floor, for there was no furniture in sight.

It was only after he quizzed me, in impeccable English, as to what I wished to purchase that he rose to his feet with a great struggle, the oak floor groaning with each movement. He stood in one spot while having me turn this way and that in front of him while he measured me with a long cord with equidistant knots. He made no notes as to my dimensions except in his mind.

The measuring chore completed, he plopped to a sitting position and beckoned me to do likewise. He showed me bits and pieces of the cloth he had available, and I made my selections. I ordered several custom-made tropical weight suits: $4.50 for white duck and $7.50 for sharkskin. Since I was not a tourist and had to leave promptly for Masbate, Lo Chin gave me two-day service. He also fitted me immediately with a lightweight shirt and slacks from his stock.

I was sorry I couldn't stay longer in Manila. It was a fascinating city of gaudy and pretentious buildings side by side with nipa palm hovels and tin shacks; well-stocked department stores with shabbily dressed adults and nearly-naked children on the adjoining sidewalks; Cadillacs and Austins sharing the streets with calesas.

And I was fascinated with its cemetery, huge and centuries old, where everyone in this city of extreme contrasts was, ultimately, equal.

two

MASBATE

The news that shocked us all reached us the next day. The Japanese had already attacked the Philippines and had destroyed almost all of our planes while on the ground, primarily at Clark Field on Luzon. Similar strikes had wiped out our air arm at other airfields as well.

The *Argus* was small, dirty, and burned soft coal, the smoke and soot finding its way into every crevice. She steamed out of the harbor and across the bay, then through the North Channel minefield in a mamma-duck-and-goslings file with several other ships under the guidance of an escort yacht. After passing Corregidor Island, each ship went its separate way.

Our route was to the southeast through the Verde Island Passage separating Luzon and Mindoro islands, then between Mindoro and Marinduque islands and across the Sibuyan Sea to Aroroy on the northeast coast of Masbate Island, the port which served the main mining camp of Masbate Consolidated at Rio Guinibatan. This route would soon become the never-to-be-forgotten path where naval history was made—where for three years U.S. Navy submarines lurked below the surface to sink Japanese ships as they sailed from Manila, headed for the San Bernardino Strait and the Philippine Sea.

The first-class passenger list consisted of seven Caucasians, all employees of Masbate Consolidated, and about fifteen well-to-do Filipinos. There were several hundred deck passengers who ate what-

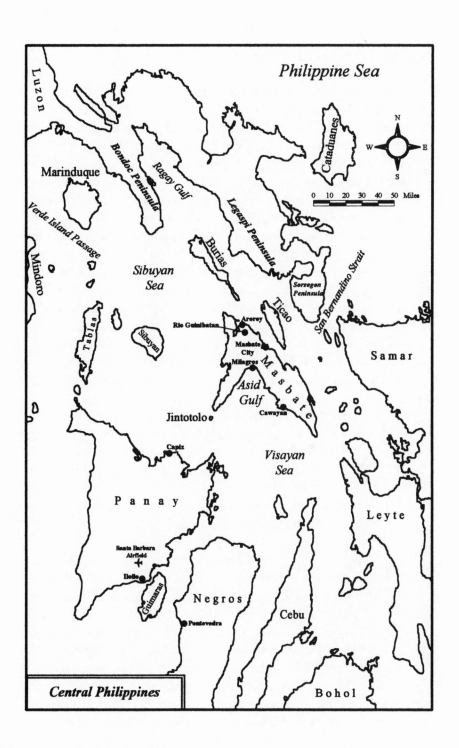

Central Philippines

ever food they brought on board with them and slept wherever space was available.

The first-class staterooms were only slightly larger than clothes closets and contained two double-deck bunks. This made little difference however, as none of us used this stuffy, humid space for anything except to store our baggage. Soon after we set sail, the ship's captain, a Filipino, told us that canvas cots had been placed on the bridge for us to use—our resting and sleeping quarters for the next two days. These dormitory-style accommodations were quite satisfactory, considering the alternative of the private cabins.

Meals were served to the first-class passengers at a long table set under an awning on the main deck, and in spite of the soot-collecting crevices on the ship, the food appeared to be clean and was very tasty. However, the method of serving was, to say the least, strange. A stack of about six plates made up each place setting, a soup dish on top, flanked by an array of silverware. As each course was served and eaten, the top dish or plate and its used cutlery were removed, exposing a clean plate on which the next course was served from kettle or platter. When the bare table appeared, the meal was over.

Upon arrival at Masbate Island, the *Argus* anchored offshore in the bay at the town of Aroroy. We were taken ashore by lighter, a small supply boat, then carried in a company-owned automobile to the mine camp at Rio Guinibatan, located about four kilometers to the south. There I was introduced to about fifteen employees who lived in the staff house, assigned a room, and on the next day entered into my duties as foreman of the Colorado Mine.

When compared by tonnage of crude ore mined and milled, Masbate Consolidated was the largest gold mining company in the Philippines, but the gold content of the ore was very low and Masbate's total gold production was exceeded by several other Philippine mines. Most of its ore came from the Panique Mine, a large low-grade deposit mined by the open-cut method. Drag-line shovels, Caterpillar tractors, front-end loaders, Carry-Alls, and a fleet of dump trucks stripped the overlying soil and piled it into man-made mountains adjacent to the work area, exposing the ore-bearing strata. The ore was then dug out and hauled to the mill, where it was crushed and the gold-bearing chunks separated from the debris in giant centrifuges. Almost three thousand native laborers worked at this strip mine under direction of forty gang foremen, of which half were Filipinos, the rest American, English, Russian, and German expatriates.

The Colorado Mine, my assignment, was an old, abandoned underground operation that the management had decided to reopen in an attempt to raise the overall quality of its ore. They expected this mine to produce, eventually, at least one thousand tons of high-grade ore per day.

This was a drift mine. Its main tunnel was a horizontal bore extending more than a half-mile into a large mountain. Diesel-powered trains of large mine cars hauled the ore from the face of the bore out to the ore mill, where the gold-bearing rock was crushed and the gold extracted.

The mining operations took place in a honeycomb of caverns dug above the main tunnel toward the crown of the mountain. There, blasting charges of dynamite were set off several times a day to break up the rock formations. Then the broken rock and ore mixture was shoveled or carted to large ore-passes, chutes cut into the rock to drop the ore down into the mine cars. The expected daily tonnage was never obtained, primarily because the main ore chute became clogged frequently, and mining had to be suspended until the clog was blasted loose and the chute cleared in an unending struggle to keep the ore running. No doubt this problem could have been cured in time, but for the appearance on the scene of Japanese troops.

About a hundred native miners were employed on each of three shifts under the supervision of a Filipino *capataz*, obviously a bastardization of the word "captain," and three assistants on each shift. It was my duty to plan each day's operations, observe the work and check the safety. And, of course, I had to perform the unceasing paperwork. It was not greatly different from my previous jobs and, except for the language difficulty and my being unaccustomed to the large amount of hand labor involved in each operation, things proceeded normally. But my pay was much better.

The mine office was located at the top of about one hundred steps. It was also midway up an inclined tram line, parallel pairs of rails on which two flat cars moved simultaneously in opposite directions. Pulled by cables from a hoist at the top, the flat cars carried supplies to another part of the mine. At the bottom of the tram line was a sign, *"Dili Sabokay sa Bagon,"* which translates to "Do Not Ride the Wagon." My understanding of this phrase covered my entire command of the native language for several months. The sign was universally ignored. No one ever walked if a car was available for riding.

From my office window, I could look out on a large employee wash room, a fifteen-foot-square concrete floor, shielded from the hot sun by a galvanized iron roof and open on four sides. In each corner was a shower head, fed with tepid water pumped from a nearby stream. All day long, women came there to wash clothes and to bathe. Much of my spare time was spent watching this very intriguing operation. Bearing a large bundle of dirty clothes on their heads and wearing only a wraparound garment like a sarong, the women, with children of all ages in tow, would come there to socialize while awaiting a turn under a shower head. As one became available, a woman would spread her laundry on the floor beneath it. With bare feet and a large wooden paddle she would knead soapy water into the pile. After rinsing out the soap, she would bundle the wet laundry and stack it to one side. Finishing the job took about thirty minutes. Then, surrounded by her nude children, she would take a bath.

Now the sarong became a personal shower curtain. While one hand clasped the edges of the curtain together securely above the breasts, the other hand soaped and rinsed. All the while the children cavorted around her, ducking in and out of the curtain. In many hours of watching, I never saw any variation in this routine, nor did I ever see the sarong fall, although it usually appeared to be on the verge. Workmen passing by would stop to converse with the bathers, and when the work shift ended, the men took over the showers.

The foreigners who still had their families with them lived in houses in the mining camp. Several men had sent their families back to the States and now lived with us in the staff house with its private rooms and community bathroom. Although the employees' houses had kitchens, most of the families took their meals in the staff house dining room, which featured American cuisine and a well-stocked bar that operated on the honor system. This room served as our recreation area in the evenings. There we congregated for card playing, checkers and other board games, reading, crafts, or just for relaxation and conversation. Much of our time was spent listening to news broadcasts from Manila and speculating on the probability of war, which led to almost unceasing discussions about whether absent families should be sent for, or families present should be sent home.

Almost weekly, we had parties at the tennis court or at one of the nearby mines. Frequently we organized swimming parties at the beach. Despite the popular impression of life in the tropics romanticized in stories and films, we did very little heavy drinking. Most of our imbibing was accompanied by poker dice games to see who would be stuck with the tab.

My morning of 8 December was no different from any other Monday morning: early breakfast; a short walk to the Colorado Mine; the ride up the inclined tram line; a couple of hours spent in going through the mine, giving instructions in simple "bastard Americano." Necessary work, but rather boring. But that day the boredom ended. Life changed. Drastically.

I was back in my office working on the time sheets when Graham Nelson, our very young American geologist rushed in, somewhat breathless.

"Just heard a flash over the radio that the Japs bombed Pearl Harbor this morning!"

"This morning?" I asked. "Do much damage?"

"Don't know. Only got the flash. I had to come up here with these assays so I couldn't wait for any more dope."

I wasn't worried. Hawaii was an ocean away, I reasoned, and my only concern was what was happening in the Philippines. At Masbate Consolidated, we had enough mining supplies for almost two years' operations. We had plenty of dynamite and blasting caps, and a tanker had just delivered a full cargo of fuel oil and gasoline. We probably had a good stock of stateside food supplies, but if not we could switch to Filipino chow. We wouldn't go hungry, and the native foods would probably be interesting.

"Hell, Graham," I said, "even if the Japs start trouble here, it will be a short war. Everybody knows that."

So Graham and I dropped the subject of war and went to studying the assays.

A short while later, on a hunch, I wired our company's Manila office requesting that they cable any money due me to my wife in the States. A few days later, Dot received the money. That evening, several other men tried unsuccessfully to do the same; all cable facilities had been closed down.

In the evening, over the dice games, we discussed the situation. We were optimistic. Reports from Pearl Harbor didn't sound too bad. Maybe the Japanese had dropped bombs on a few ships and maybe there were some casualties, but if they tried to attack the Philippines it would only take a week or ten days for our fleet to get here. In a couple of months the Japanese would be licked and our operations would be back to normal. We wouldn't be affected.

All out war? No way. We agreed that Masbate Consolidated's operations would continue as usual.

The news that shocked us all came the next day. The Japanese had already attacked the Philippines and had destroyed almost all of our planes while on the ground, primarily at Clark Field on Luzon Island. Similar strikes had wiped out our air arm at other airfields as well.

Two days later we learned that Japanese bombers had wrecked the U.S. Naval Base at Cavite, in Manila Bay, and Japanese troops had landed at Aparri, on the north coast of Luzon, and at Vigan, on its west coast.

We became more concerned seventy-two hours later on hearing the Japanese had landed at Legaspi, near the southern tip of Luzon, and attempted to land at Lingayen. Apparently, very little was being done to stop them, although our troops had successfully repulsed the landing at Lingayen. But we knew that most of our troops were in the Manila area, and rapid troop movement from there to the landing areas was difficult. It was in Manila that we'd give them hell.

But the Japanese were moving in fast. In less than a week they had invaded central Luzon at three places, including Legaspi.

And Legaspi was only fifty air miles from Masbate!

Our mining operations continued as usual, but not for long. The employees began to grumble when the company missed the payroll of the fifteenth, for the money hadn't arrived from Manila. We solved the problem temporarily by issuing scrip, to be honored at the company store. All the scrip was immediately spent and the store's stock was depleted in a hurry.

The grumbling increased, and within a few days most of the men quit working. There wasn't much sense in working for scrip that can't be spent, they contended. Soon we had less than half a crew on the work site each day. Production dropped, but mining went on. With the workers who did appear, we set up a seven-day-a-week schedule.

Until 18 December, we had seen no sign of war except for a definite increase in air traffic, unidentified and flying quite high. On that afternoon, however, one lone four-engine bomber—Japanese, we all agreed—flew fairly low over the mine, pursued by several fighter planes. The bomber was flying an erratic course, seeking cover in the many low, fleecy clouds. It wasn't much of an aerial battle, but at least it gave us something concrete to talk about over our drinks that evening. We were sure our planes had been able to shoot down that lone Jap bomber.

At about eleven o'clock that night, a phone call came in from Milagros, a small *barrio*, an outlying village, about twenty miles to the south, at the head of Asid Gulf on the west coast of the island. The bomber we had seen had made a forced landing in a nearby rice paddy and several of the crew were wounded. Would we send transportation to bring the men to the mine, asked the caller? The plane was one of our B-17's, not the Japanese bomber we had believed it to be. The war was getting closer.

The truck we dispatched to Milagros returned early the next morning with the seven crew members. After treatment at the mine hospital, where shell fragments were laboriously and painfully picked from their anatomies, six of the men were given rooms in the guest house. The seventh had been shot through the ankle and stayed hospitalized.

Capt. Jack Adams, the pilot, was a hero—almost a god—to his crew. Without exception, they maintained that he was "the best damned pilot in the world" and but for his skill, not a man among them would be alive.

Lieutenant Scheiber, the navigator (I cannot recall his first name), showed me a list of the geographic coordinates for all Japanese airfields on Formosa. He had compiled this information on the morning of 8 December, immediately after he learned of the Japanese attack on Pearl Harbor, in preparation for what he saw as the most logical retaliatory move. He never got to use it. Their plane, instead of participating in an offensive operation, had been one of a few moved to bases on other islands before the Japanese onslaught on Clark Field. The failure to bomb the Japanese installations on Formosa was, to him, a major command error, and he was very vocal in his condemnation of the U.S. Army Air Corps brass.

Lieutenant Scheiber proved to be a professional-level gambler who kept a low-stakes poker game going day and night. He easily recognized that there wasn't any money to be picked up among us for, like all the other employees, we hadn't been paid either. I was probably the richest man in the mine crew and my total stake couldn't have been more than thirty pesos. Too, he probably would not have gotten any kicks out of fleecing a bunch of amateurs. So he made it a fun game, and when he left none of us was any richer or any poorer. Scheiber had controlled the games with a combination of poker skill and sleight-of-hand, and no one was hurt financially. And when it became necessary later for me to take off toward the hills, that thirty pesos was my entire fortune.

It was still business as usual during working hours. But at social gatherings, such as the Saturday night parties at the tennis court, things were getting tense. The Filipinos were becoming troublesome, occasionally insolent, for the company now owed them more than two weeks' salary and the scrip was worthless.

On Christmas Day, the staff followed an established custom of attending an open house at the manager's hilltop home. Barney Faust, the manager, provided plenty of food and drink, and the day began with everyone reasonably happy and carefree, with little thought being given to the future. In the late afternoon, however, an impromptu meeting developed, and we began making evacuation plans, at least for the women and children. The air corps men had made contact with their unit and all except the injured radio operator, who remained in the hospital, had left for Panay Island in a small native *vinta,* a sailboat with outriggers. Since this method of travel seemed to be available without interference from the Japanese, most of the men whose wives and families were still with them saw this as a way to get them closer to the protection of the military. It would be a risky venture, they knew, but for them to remain on Masbate Island, where no semblance of military protection existed, was not practical. Perhaps from Panay they could be evacuated to safety. How? They did not know—but even fruitless action would be better than inaction, they reasoned. Barney Faust agreed, saying that anyone wishing to leave could do so, but he couldn't provide them with any money. With the exception of Mrs. Faust, Rose Preiser (the school teacher), and one or two others, most of the women, along with several men, left on 28 December.

Work at the mine went limping along but, due to the lack of laborers and the "what the hell" attitude of most of the Americans, very little was accomplished. Any optimism we had gave way to caution with each passing day. We reminded each other that establishing Philippine army garrisons throughout the smaller islands such as ours would take time. Suppose the Japanese arrived before our troops. What then?

At the staff house in the evenings, drinking became more common. Rolling dice for the drinks became an every night occurrence, but it was no longer a carefree game. Pocket money was scarce, and the games grew more competitive. Tensions mounted, especially between the Americans and the English. We Americans bristled at criticism of MacArthur and his conduct of the war, while jokes about the British, especially those with reference to the Queen, were a "no-no." Everyone's nerves were on edge, a condition that was rapidly becoming worse. Considering the stress we were under, however, we all got along surprisingly well, and there were very few actions beyond occasional harsh words.

We spent New Year's Eve, too, at Faust's home, and as the evening wore on our moods darkened, as did the night. Listening to the radio, we heard the newscaster announce that Manila had fallen to the Japanese. The station was going off the air, he said, and he ended his broadcast with a prayer for help and guidance. When he finished, there was dead silence among us. How long would it be until the rest of the islands were lost to the invaders? And when that happened, where would *we* be?

three

EVACUATION

I was lying on a hard bamboo platform only a few feet off the ground, in a small cleared area carved out of a dense tropical forest. Overhead was a canopy of jungle growth that, even in midday, would have sealed the sun and sky from view. At this midnight hour the only light reflecting from the canopy came from our campfire.

New Year's Day dawned bright and sunny, a holiday at the mine. We all lazed about, not talking very much. In the afternoon, several Japanese planes flew low overhead, by now a very common occurrence. With nothing to do and nothing happening, we all went to bed early, depressed and worried.

About midnight, I was awakened by Graham Nelson, the young geologist, bursting into the room.

"The Japs have landed in Masbate City and are coming this way. We're pulling out!"

"Where did you get the news?" I asked, as I struggled to rouse myself.

"Just got a phone call from Masbate," he answered, and ran to wake up the others. Masbate City was the provincial capital, some thirty miles southeast of us. A good, mostly-paved coastal highway connected the two towns.

Although we all knew we might have to run for the hills at a moment's notice, no one had made any definite preparations for evacuation. Now, we were suddenly being forced out, with perhaps two hours at most to pack food and gear for the move into the hills and the unknown beyond.

Everyone had a different idea about where to go and what to do. Most of us agreed that the best bet was to head for the IXL Mine, one of our company's operations twelve kilometers southeast, a few miles off the coastal highway at the edge of the *bondoc*, the forest jungle. Because of our joint weekly parties, we knew all the Americans who lived there. We decided to make that the first evacuation point. However, to get there meant that most of the way we had to travel toward the Japanese landing area, on the same highway the enemy would be using if they were to move toward the Aroroy harbor. Then we would leave the highway, turning west toward the IXL mine.

I teamed up with Ken Hansen, the mine foreman of another division of Masbate Consolidated. Tall, skinny, and even-tempered, Ken was one of the several married men whose wives had remained with them at Masbate. But several weeks before Christmas, Mrs. Hansen and another company wife, Mrs. Homer Mann, had gone to Manila on a shopping trip and were trapped there when Luzon came under siege. Both husbands were frantically seeking ways to rescue them— they had even contemplated going to the city to search for them until a refugee from Manila arrived on Masbate and told of the chaotic situation encountered by Americans there. The man suggested waiting until the Manila situation had a chance to stabilize. Reluctantly, Ken and Homer decided to accept his advice.

Ken's house was well stocked with food, and for about an hour he and I frantically packed some personal belongings, food, and cooking utensils into makeshift knapsacks and canvas bags, preparing for an indefinite stay in the jungle. At around one o'clock in the morning, we left for IXL in his car—a junker he had unsuccessfully tried to convert into an all-terrain vehicle.

We covered the seven miles of highway to the turnoff leading to the IXL mine without incident. We didn't know if the Japanese were planning to move northward along the highway, but we hoped that if they did they would wait until daylight to do so. At every curve we expected to be met by gunfire. We arrived safely at IXL at about 2 A.M. Since the road toward the jungle ended there, Ken stashed his car in a mine shed.

The IXL camp was in confusion. The Americans who lived there had already moved toward the hills. The native employees, milling about in large, unruly mobs, had broken into the company store and bodega, stripping them completely. Surly and hostile, and armed with *bolos*, machetes, they obviously resented our presence. This attitude was so contrary to our good rapport in the past. We began to fear that all the Filipinos were turning against Americans and intended to support the Japanese. This proved, later, to be a false impression. They were upset, surprised, and bewildered to see all of us leaving them unprotected and helpless, running at the first cry of "Japanese!"

Loaded down with our enormous backpacks, and more than a little frightened, Ken and I trudged through the camp, hunting the trail to the XYZ mine, located deeper in the mountains to the west. Before we reached the camp's outer limits, a short, husky native, about eighteen years old, approached us, bowed, and said, "Sirs. You will take me with you?"

We were already faltering under our outsized burdens. Our gear was simply too heavy and bulky for us to handle. Also, Ken and I knew absolutely nothing about jungle life, native foods, or woodcraft. With a minimum of discussion, we agreed that having this man, Undet, join us was our first stroke of luck.

An Igorot who, in a spirit of adventure, had left his home near Baguio, Luzon, to see the world, Undet had been at IXL for less than a month. He was almost as much in a foreign land as we, for his native dialect did not translate easily into Visayan. In fact, he could speak English far better than he could speak the local dialect.

Language barriers exist throughout the islands. While English is taught in the schools and is quite prevalent among the young in the larger towns and villages, it is not a universal language. Tagalog is extensively used throughout Luzon. It is completely different from Visayan, which prevails in the central islands—those south of Luzon and north of Mindanao—and Mindanao Visayan, again differing considerably, which is spoken on that island and to the south. In addition, the tribes living in the hills and jungles and on isolated islands have clung to their ancient tongues.

Rearranging our gear into three packs reduced our loads to more manageable burdens. We then set out on the trail through the mountainous jungle. Up and up we trudged and stumbled in pitch-black darkness. Only occasionally did we use our flashlights, and then just for a few seconds, because we feared the Japanese might spot the light, even though we were sure we were miles from the nearest enemy troops. Despite the reduced loads we were carrying, Ken and I were near exhaustion when we finally reached XYZ at about seven in the morning. Undet was hardly breaking a sweat.

XYZ was a small prospect, an area where many test pits were being checked for ore quality to determine if a full-fledged mining operation there would be worthwhile. Owned by IXL, it was operated by Dick Weisner, an American we had met at Masbate Consolidated's social gatherings, and his Filipina wife. They welcomed us, gave us a hearty breakfast, and Dick suggested that we stay with them. He told us that others from Masbate's mines—Louise and Harold Spencer and Homer Mann—had preceded us to his house by two hours, but they had continued on to a cabin about two kilometers farther along the trail. After some discussion, we declined his invitation to stay, and after a short rest we followed along behind the Spencers and Mann, as we still felt the Japanese were much too close for comfort.

By now, Ken and I had decided that our trip to this mine was definitely a mistake. With 20/20 hindsight we thought we should have headed directly to the west coast and from there traveled by vinta to Panay Island, where American troops were based.

After finding the Spencers and Homer Mann, we again reviewed our options. We agreed that Panay should be our destination, but Harold had sprained his ankle quite badly and probably wouldn't be able to walk for several days. They urged Ken and me to go on ahead. They would follow after Harold became mobile. We were without a map of the island, so we guessed as to the best and shortest route to the coast. Then Ken, Undet, and I continued on.

Our route lay along a stream and, as there was no trail, we were obliged to follow its bed. Luckily, the water was very low and, at the expense of constantly wet feet, we made good time. About four in the afternoon, we came upon an old, abandoned woodcutter's shack. Tired, lame, and sore, we decided to spend the night there. This was the first of many nights I would spend in the jungle.

The shack was simply a four-foot by seven-foot bamboo platform, built on stakes about five feet above the ground, covered with a dilapidated grass roof. Although Undet had previously proved his worth as a packer, he now proved that he was no less valuable as a woodsman. He cut new bamboo to patch the floor on which Ken and I were to sleep, repaired the roof with large *anahow*, or palm leaves, gathered wood, built a fire, and cooked rice in my hard-boiled aluminum hat, which for a long time would serve alternately as a head covering, water bucket, and rice kettle. We didn't mind how or what Undet did. Ken and I not only knew nothing of jungle life, we were almost too exhausted even to move.

Undet slept on the ground under us, and was continually being awakened to "Put more green wood on the fire, the mosquitoes are eating us up," or "Take the wood off the fire, it's so smoky we can't breathe." Morning finally arrived, but we were still too tired to move. The entire day was spent doing nothing. That night we again fought the mosquitoes and smoke. The following morning, however, we were sufficiently rested, and we took off again for the coast, and for the island of Panay.

The stream we were following soon began to get too wide and deep for wading and we were forced to take to the bank. With no trail, it proved to be very tough going. Occasionally we came to *caingins*, burnt-out clearings in the jungle for farms, but all of them were abandoned and we feared that the Japanese had driven the occupants away. We were paranoid now about the presence of the Japanese, imagining them to be everywhere. Around noon we saw several Filipinos, but by now we believed they were our enemies as well and we took evasive measures to avoid them.

Soon we left the forest and entered the Masbate plains that cover much of the southern half of the island. These seas of cogon grass—plants ranging from five to seven feet tall with long, narrow, razor-sharp leaves—extended for mile after mile over rolling hills. Large herds of Brahma cattle grazed there, feeding on the new shoots growing at the base of the plants. There were no trails for us to follow. This was range land, with nothing but grass and cattle in sight to the horizon. We were without a map or a compass, but even with these items we would have been lost in this territory bereft of landmarks.

We had no choice but to walk in the direction the sun told us was the way to Asid Gulf. Once there, we would follow the coast until we came to a town, hopefully a town without a Japanese garrison. Even then, we knew we would be hard-pressed to find a boatman who would sail us to Panay, for our pooled wealth was less than fifty pesos—twenty-five American dollars. Ours was a very bleak outlook.

As we crossed a low ridge, we spotted a seeming oasis in this hot, dry sea of grass. A cluster of palms and what appeared to be greener vegetation lay several kilometers ahead. Although the day was rapidly getting along toward sunset, we decided to press on, hoping this would be a good place to bed down for the night. As we drew nearer, we could see the outlines of several rather large buildings. Perhaps this was the home of the rancher whose cattle we had met up with on the range. But once more, we asked ourselves the same trite question: Will we encounter friend or foe?

We decided to approach the place after dark, and if conditions seemed normal, rouse the owners and ask for directions. Concealed by the tall grass, sometimes crawling on our bellies, we reached a point on the road only a hundred yards from the house. Everything appeared quiet and peaceful. Which one of us was to go up to the door? We decided to draw straws, then changed our minds.

"What the hell," I said. "Let's stay together." All three of us walked up to the house and knocked on the door.

A wonderful welcome awaited us. The owner, a Spaniard, and his Filipina wife greeted us like long-lost relatives. They had spoken to no one from the outside world since the Japanese attack on the islands and were anxious to hear first-hand news from the capital city area.

While we scrubbed off the grime from our several days of hiking, the señora prepared dinner: chicken, beef, pork, milk, eggs, many vegetables, and a kind of freshwater snail. We were ravenous, and the meal was wonderful—in retrospect, better than any I could remember eating at the mine. Of course, I had never been that hungry at the mine.

Our host and hostess were obviously well educated. They spoke the native tongue, Visayan, which Undet tried with passably good results. Ken used a bit of his high school Spanish, and that worked to some extent. I had only English at my disposal, but it became our best common language of the night.

Our host and hostess told us they resided in Cawayan, a small town some twenty-five miles to the south. But when they heard of the Japanese landings on Luzon, they immediately moved from the town to this ranch, normally run by their hired overseer, and visited by them only on rare occasions. Being much older than we were, they said they feared they would not be able to move out quickly if the Japanese should land in their town. This was their *buckwheation*, a term signifying a hiding place, derived from the way the Filipinos pronounced the English word "evacuate."

We talked for hours, sitting around the dining room table, under the eerie light of coconut oil lamps. The señor gave us directions to the town, names of people to contact there, and the name of a boatman who would carry us to Panay. And that night we had soft beds to sleep in—with pillows!

It was nearly noon before we started the trek to Cawayan the next day. When we arrived there, we got more disturbing news: The report of the Japanese landing at Masbate City had been a false alarm! A renegade gang of dishonest Filipinos, mostly Masbate Consolidated employees, had phoned in the entirely untrue news simply to start a mass evacuation of the Americans. They certainly succeeded. This, in turn, led to the riotous looting of bodegas and homes and gave the ringleaders a chance to loot the mine safe where almost a million pesos worth of gold bullion was stored.

four

BACK TO THE MINE

Free at last, I made a solemn promise to never again willingly allow myself to be taken by the Japanese. I kept that vow.

The next morning Ken Hanson and I found a car and driver to take us back to the mine. Undet decided to stay at Cawayan. The vehicle was a battered and beaten mid-1920s vintage, seven-passenger Packard touring car that had long ago been stripped of its cloth top and the collapsible tubular framework which had supported it. In fact, even the windshield and its supports were only a memory, as was any semblance of the original leather upholstery. But its engine had survived and worked surprisingly well considering that for years it was lubricated with coconut oil and fueled with a mixture of gasoline and distilled nipa palm juice.

The road was little more than a jungle trail, and at times we had to widen it by hacking away the overgrowth with bolos. There were no bridges over the streams, and we forded them as best we could.

Eventually we reached one of the better roads that served the mining property. Signs of looting were everywhere. What a mess! While the organized gang had blasted the door off the safe and stolen the gold bullion, free-lance looters had cleaned out everything else.

No house or staff room remained untouched and virtually everything was taken: pictures, letters, clothing—even old shoes and dirty, worn-out clothing. Electrical fixtures had been torn from the walls and ceilings; pipes and fixtures had been yanked out. All had been carried away in stolen company trucks, now wrecked and scattered throughout the area. But the natives professed innocence of any wrongdoing.

"Everything was taken to keep it from the Japs only, Sair!" they explained.

The two succeeding weeks were spent in a mostly futile effort to salvage trucks and put them in running condition, and in a search of Filipino houses in an equally futile attempt to recover personal belongings. A few people were lucky enough to recover some of their personal effects. In a very few isolated cases, items were returned voluntarily.

Early in the morning on the day we returned, Japanese planes had flown low over the camp, dropping leaflets that said the Emperor's forces were rapidly securing control of Masbate Island. Several of the Americans, mostly those with families, hurriedly headed for the hills again, but the majority of us remained at the mine.

Later the same morning, 7 January 1942, many Filipinos came through our camp from Aroroy, the port four kilometers away, with the news that a shipload of Japanese soldiers was coming ashore. The Filipinos were fleeing to the homes of relatives in rural areas. Another exodus of Americans started immediately. Most left in cars, although there were no roads in the hills and cars would soon prove useless. Ken and I, having had enough jungle life for a while, simply went to a partially cultivated hillside a half-mile from camp where we sat for several hours, the camp buildings in sight below us. Several planes flew low over the area. There were no signs of life at the mine. Except for a few diehards, all the Filipinos had fled.

Early in the afternoon we noticed some stirring in the town below. Soon several Filipinos came up the hill and told us that the Japanese had all re-boarded the ship at Aroroy and left without coming to the mine.

Ken Hansen and I returned to the staff house, joining Homer Mann and Bill Rowe, manager of IXL. We were the only Americans there. Ken and Homer wrestled with all sorts of fruitless plans for evacuation, for their wives were still in Manila—or somewhere—

probably in the hands of the Japanese. Any course they might choose, short of heading for Manila and finding them, at whatever the cost, would be unsatisfactory. How would they ever be reunited? They finally agreed, very reluctantly, that their own survival was most important just then.

Ken and I decided to look for a vehicle to use when we had to depart again. Any vehicle would do, but we preferred one small enough and tough enough to fit and cope with the rough jungle trails. We searched unsuccessfully for one of the small, gasoline-powered ore loaders—not much more than powered wheelbarrows—used inside the narrow confines of the mine shafts. The only vehicle we found in running condition was a one-ton cab-over-engine Chevrolet truck. It didn't meet the specifications of an off-the-road vehicle, to be sure, especially since its brakes were shot, but it was better than nothing. Since I had located the truck, I claimed ownership. That evening, to keep it from being stolen, I transposed some of the ignition wires before parking it in a garage near the staff house. It would spit and backfire occasionally, but getting it to run would be a time-consuming job for even the most determined and mechanically inclined thief.

Later, the four of us discussed possible escape plans. We were all jittery and as the night wore on we became more so. About midnight, we heard yelling from the direction of the Philippine Constabulary (PC) barracks, which were located a short distance from the staff house. There, some twenty or thirty Japanese civilians were interned along with several Germans, including Goldie Goldhammer, the shift boss who worked with me at the Colorado mine. During the recent false alarm and looting spree, two Americans who had remained in camp during the whole event supplied the prisoners with food and then persuaded the PC's not to shoot them. As a result, the prison inmates, Japanese as well as Germans, became our allies although, as prisoners, there was little they could do to help us.

Ken went to investigate. He returned almost immediately to say that all the lights were on in the barracks and that lots of people were milling around, both outside and inside the barbed-wire fence surrounding it. He was sure the Japanese had finally arrived.

Ken and I left to warn Homer Mann, who had returned to his house and gone to bed. We woke him, and the three of us took a circuitous route to a point above and about a hundred yards from the barracks, where we could look down into the compound. Ken was right, for there were definitely Japanese soldiers, and plenty of them, in the compound. They seemed to be reasonably calm.

We watched for almost an hour, then sneaked back to the staff house. It was vacant except for two Filipino houseboys. They told us that some time earlier a party of Japanese had arrived, talked a long time with Bill Rowe, then took him along when they left—destination unknown. Bill had told the boys that if Ken or I showed up, he wanted to see us immediately—especially *me!* The boys thought it might have to do with a "car." We decided to go to the garage where I'd parked the old truck I'd found.

Ever since our first evacuation, Ken had been carrying a small black bag containing his wife's jewelry, some silver pieces, and a .32-caliber revolver. I was carrying a small bolo in a scabbard at my waist. Halfway to the garage, we reasoned that since there were probably Japanese there, it would be very foolish to show up armed. Ken hid his revolver in some grass, I ditched my bolo, and we proceeded to the garage, a long, narrow galvanized iron building without doors, half filled with broken-down trucks. As we were about to enter, a dozen or so Japanese soldiers stepped out of the shadows and surrounded us.

"Good evening, Sirs," the leader, apparently a lieutenant, said in fair English. I suppose we answered, but I don't remember what we said. We were searched very hurriedly and haphazardly.

One of the soldiers said, "Cigarette." I gave him an opened package just as Ken set his little black bag on the ground. Roughly, the lieutenant pulled Ken away from the bag and in a hostile voice demanded, "What is?"

"Just some personal effects," Ken answered.

"Open."

"But they are personal belongings," Ken stammered.

The lieutenant gave Ken a shove; some of the soldiers raised their rifles while he repeated, "Open."

Ken stooped down and opened the bag. Pulling him away, the lieutenant knelt down, ran his hands through the bag, and after removing two packages of cigarettes from an opened carton on top, closed the bag and handed it to Ken.

"All right. You can have."

"Ken? Ham? Where are you?" called Homer suddenly from ten feet away.

We all stepped from the shadows, but the Japanese soldiers, noticing that Homer had failed to remove his bolo, presented their bayonets while moving toward him menacingly. The lieutenant stopped them.

"Why you carry big knife?" he asked Homer.

"Just to cut wood—open cans." Homer answered. Ken and I tried to explain to the lieutenant that it was only a working tool and we all carried them much of the time.

"All right," he said. "You keep."

"Any you Mr. Hamner?" he asked.

"I am," I answered, wondering what I had done to be known to him by name.

"Mr. Lowe say you can make car run. You can?"

"Yes," I said.

"You come," he ordered, and I went.

Our little group moved to the staff house. Ken and Homer went inside while I was escorted to the garage—and to my truck—by the Japanese.

Quickly, under the sharp eyes of the soldiers, I changed the wires and started the engine. All the Japanese got into the truck, the lieutenant in the front seat.

"Get in," he motioned to me. "You drive to barracks." I did as he ordered.

At the PC barracks I was taken into a large room where Bill Rowe and Harry Morrison, the manager of a small mine who had been hiding in a nearby Filipino's house, were sitting. The room was filled with Japanese soldiers and the Japanese and German civilian internees. Bill and Harry told me the Japanese were hunting for trucks to transport the prisoners and their belongings to Aroroy, where the Japanese launch was anchored. So far, my truck and a station wagon belonging to Morrison were the only vehicles they had. Bill Rowe had a passenger car, but it was too small to be of any use.

The officer in charge of the party was a pock-marked major of the marines. He could speak no English, and his interpreter was one of the Japanese internees, an ex-storekeeper from Aroroy who was now wearing a Japanese army uniform.

"The truck will run?" the major in charge asked me through the interpreter.

"Yes, sir, but it has no brakes and it is dangerous to drive," I answered.

"You will drive," he ordered. End of discussion.

They still wanted more trucks, and after considerable discussion, it was decided that Bill Rowe would drive to IXL in his passenger car and return with a truck. Morrison would go to *his* mine and put tires on a truck, making it available for use. After the two of them left, I felt very lonely—the only American among some eighty Japanese. Ken Hansen was around somewhere, but I had no idea where. To increase my apprehension, I noticed that soldiers surrounded the building and large-caliber machine guns were mounted on pipe tripods on all sides.

But I couldn't brood on my situation for long. As the soldiers loaded the truck, I asked the major to allow Goldie Goldhammer to accompany me on the trip—which became multiple trips. Surprisingly, he agreed and I felt somewhat better. At least I would have someone to talk to. But a couple more hours of waiting alone lay ahead for me.

Finally, at about five in the morning, Goldie joined me and we were ready to leave—in my old, temperamental truck loaded with baggage, civilians, and four armed guards.

As I drove along the road, lined most of the way with houses and small shops, a few Filipinos waved half-heartedly at the Japanese in the eerie dawn. Most of the houses had a white flag flying over the door; few women or children could be seen.

The road to Aroroy was downhill, winding, and quite steep, but by down-shifting into low gear I was able to keep the vehicle under control without brakes. I drove directly to the dock. Baggage and passengers were unloaded, and I started back immediately, Goldie and the guards still with me.

It was now daylight. I had not slept for more than thirty hours. I was tired, sleepy, and very nervous. As I made a left turn onto the highway, I saw the station wagon loaded with Japanese coming directly toward me. Never before had I driven in the Philippines, where traffic keeps to the left. My reflex action was to move to the right, but then I remembered the local rules of the road and swerved to the left.

The station wagon nearly went into the ditch to pass me, but its occupants laughed and waved me on.

Ahead was a steep hill that I tried unsuccessfully to climb in high gear. When I had to downshift, I missed the lower gear and my truck started to roll down the hill backwards, without brakes and with four Japanese soldiers in the back of the truck. Cramping the wheels desperately, I ran the truck onto the bank, nearly tipping it over. Now we were stuck. From a nearby native's shack, with considerable "persuasion" from the armed guards, several Filipinos with shovels came to dig us out and push us back onto the road. Then we were again on our way.

After three more round trips without incident, I was ordered to drive several of the Japanese to Morrison's place to find out why he hadn't returned with the truck. We found him struggling with mounting the last tire. When he finally finished, we all returned to the barracks, and then made one more trip to the boat with the last of the baggage, and with one more boat passenger—Goldie Goldhammer.

Upon our return to the barracks, the Filipinos, until now kept at a distance, were ordered to come close. Some five hundred gathered around the barracks steps. For the first time, I noticed that the American and Philippine flags had been lowered—replaced by a Japanese flag. I cannot describe the lost feeling this gave me. I now realized that I was no longer under the protection of the Stars and Stripes, but was one of the vanquished, under an enemy flag. I wasn't the only person who surreptitiously wiped tears from his eyes.

Ceremoniously, the Japanese major now mounted the steps, flanked by loaded and manned machine guns, several of his underling officers, and two interpreters. One of the latter would translate from Japanese to English, the other from English to Visayan. I don't remember his exact words, but the gist of his speech was:

> "The Japanese have entirely destroyed the American fleet at Pearl Harbor. We have taken Manila and most of Luzon and will soon complete the occupation of the Philippines. A free Greater East Asia is at hand. Peace and order in the Philippines must be restored under the benevolent eyes of the Japanese.
>
> "We are leaving now but we will very soon return and

reorganize the civil government. In the meantime, the mines here will reopen and you are all to return to work tomorrow morning, under the American civilians. Any refusal to work or any more robbing and looting of mine property will be punished by death."

Scattered applause followed the speech as the crowd began to leave. The Japanese flag was lowered and all but one machine gun was dismounted. A small sedan belonging to Lester Mason had been found and, driven by a Japanese soldier, was being used as a staff car by the Japanese officers. I was ordered to get someone to go to Aroroy with me to drive it back to the mine.

Meanwhile, through an interpreter, Morrison was complaining to the major that a pair of sunglasses had been stolen from his truck. He demanded that the soldiers be questioned immediately, adding rather stupidly, we thought, that the American army and navy would soon drive the Japanese out of the islands. The major bristled.

"The American fleet is totally destroyed and America itself will soon be occupied," he screamed.

I didn't like the trend of this conversation, so I left immediately, unescorted, for the staff house, to see if I could find the other driver. As I approached the building, the first thing I saw was the American flag gloriously flying from the flag pole. In the confusion, no one had lowered it and the flag had waved over the heads of the Japanese during the entire night! This was a small but very heartening incident, and one of very few for a very long time.

I found Ken Hansen, who agreed to accompany me. We returned to the barracks and, with a truckload of Japanese soldiers and machine guns, left for Aroroy. Ken and a Japanese officer shared the front seat with me.

Halfway to Aroroy, extremely sleepy and nervous, I drove off the road again, almost tipping the truck over. All the Japanese got out, pushed the truck back on the road, and we continued, with Ken driving. I had had enough. And they'd had enough of my driving.

After arriving at the wharf and unloading, most of the soldiers managed a smile and a "thank you." With his interpreter, the Japanese major came over, shook hands, and said, "Thank you. You may go now." We went.

Free at last, I made a solemn promise to never again willingly allow myself to be taken by the Japanese. I kept that vow.

Although the half-million dollars worth of gold bullion stolen from Masbate Consolidated's safe had not been recovered, about one hundred thousand dollars worth of the IXL bullion was found. Soon afterward, it was taken to Panay by Charles Smith, Harvey Weidman, and others. During their absence, we repaired several trucks and made many trips throughout the island, partly to recover loot and partly to purchase all the rice possible.

The shortage of this staple had already become serious. The natives were primarily laborers around the various mines, and they depended on the company stores for their food supplies. Small garden plots were being planted as rapidly as possible, but it would be several months before they yielded any food, and even then the gardens would supply only vegetables that supplemented the rice diet. Growing rice requires large tracts of farmland, carefully constructed dikes, weirs, pumps—not exactly a backyard garden activity. Too, rice was a staple for the Japanese army, and they would soon be seizing all they could find. It was imperative that we collect and stash it as securely as possible.

On 15 January we received word that Charlie Smith was expected to return from Panay the following morning with a boatload of rice and canned goods. Early in the morning we headed across the island to Milagros with several trucks to transport the supplies to the camp. Upon our arrival, we found the eighty-foot-long tug about a half-mile off shore, hard and fast on a sand bar, hidden under palm fronds, branches, and grass. Smith had directed the camouflage operation and insisted that from the air it looked like a small island. To us it looked like a tug camouflaged with palm fronds, branches, and grass. It remained stuck on the bar for several hours until the tide came in and floated the craft. Smith then moved it up a small stream for unloading.

The boat ran aground again within twenty feet of the bank, in water three feet deep. From there the cargo was unloaded by hand—or rather by head. A horde of barefooted, diminutive Filipinos, attired in abaca cloth shorts, waded from the boat to the shore in a steady stream, each bearing a sack of rice on his head. They dropped the sacks into one of our trucks and returned for another sack. The cargo was then transported to the bodegas at the mine camp.

Passengers on the boat were thirty Filipino soldiers, under the command of a third lieutenant, on a mission to recover more of the stolen gold bullion. They were also to return with bulldozers and dynamite from the mine. These were to be used in airfield construction. The soldiers remained at the mine for two days. They searched hundreds of houses and interrogated many people. No trace of the gold was found.

On the evening of the second day's unloading, we again heard a rumor of a Japanese landing at Masbate City. Ken Hansen and Homer Mann decided to drive there in Ken's car to check the validity of the rumor. Meanwhile, the lieutenant in charge of the Filipino troops demanded that he and his men be driven immediately to the west coast, where the tug was waiting to return them to Panay. Despite my earlier demonstrations of a complete lack of skill behind the wheel, I was drafted into the chauffeuring job.

Driving a three-ton flatbed truck, with the soldiers and Tom Sawyer (not of Mark Twain fame but another of our mining companions) in the back, and Athol Y. "Chick" Smith in front with me, I followed Ken and Homer toward Masbate City. After traveling some twenty kilometers south along the main highway, Ken and Homer continued toward the city, while I turned to the west on a narrow, often swampy, seldom traveled dirt road.

Like most of the recovered vehicles, the truck had poor brakes and one weak, flickering headlight—very inadequate for night driving in a jungle. The first five kilometers went fairly well. I successfully negotiated three long wooden bridges decked with longitudinal two-inch by twelve-inch runners—so narrow that the outside dual tires hung over both edges. On the fourth bridge of similar construction, my "skill" and my luck deserted me. Disaster struck.

I drove up over a sharp pitch directly in front of my flickering headlight and negotiated a slight curve leading to bridge number four, a forty-foot-long span about ten feet above a dry creek bed. Halfway across, I felt the left front wheel start to slip to the side. Very slowly, the truck dropped off the bridge and landed upside down in the stream bed. The fuel tank under the front seat ruptured, saturating me and my clothing with gallons of gasoline. I vividly remember shouting over and over, "Don't light any matches! Don't smoke!" No one did, thank God.

Chick Smith and I crawled out of the cab, while other men crawled out from under the vehicle. The partially crushed cab top lay flat on the creek's bottom; the back of the truck bed hung partway up the bank. Sawyer was pinned to the ground by wreckage across his hips, but his head and upper body were outside and free. One Filipino soldier was crushed under the edge of the truck bed and probably died instantly.

Frantically, we worked to free the two men, but with no tools it seemed an endless job. There was no jack in the truck, and we had no pry bars. We finally ripped some plank runners off the bridge and used them as levers. It took us at least an hour to free the men.

Everyone was bruised and sore—some may have had broken bones—and Tom was in severe pain. The soldiers, very antagonistic, stared menacingly at me. I can't say that I blamed them; I felt responsible for the mess. And to us, the soldier's death was the first fatality associated with the war.

There were no houses nearby, and as someone had to go for help, I volunteered to walk back to the junction to see if I could find someone. It was a long and disagreeable walk, with no moon, a chill made more so by the gasoline evaporating from my clothing, and I was very jittery. Eventually, and still with no houses in sight, I arrived at the junction and sat down to rest, trying to think of my next move. It seemed sensible to walk south to the home of a Spanish-Filipino acquaintance, about six kilometers away.

As I started walking south, I saw car lights approaching from the direction of Masbate City. Friends or enemy Japanese? There was no way of knowing. Hesitantly, I hailed the car from the side of the road and heard Ken Hansen ask, "What's wrong, Ham?" The Japanese hadn't landed. It was another rumor.

Relieved, I climbed into their car and we drove to the scene of the accident. Learning that there was no danger of a Japanese attack, the lieutenant decided that his party would stay where they were, bury their comrade in the morning, then proceed on foot to the west coast.

Tom and Chick got into the car with us, and we five Americans returned to the mine, where an examination by the local doctor revealed that Tom Sawyer had no broken bones or serious injuries. He was soon walking around again, although he limped for several weeks.

The next week to ten days were spent in what became a daily routine. Part of our time was spent hunting for food and stolen belongings; the rest went to caring for the mine's tools and equipment. All the hand tools—air compressors, jack hammers, hoses, small hoists, and the like—we assembled in a central bodega, cleaned, and stored. Large compressors, diesel engines, generators, and other heavy equipment were given a protective coating of grease to prevent rust. Although much of the work may have been useless, it kept us busy and left little time for personal arguments or useless worrying.

Late in the afternoon of 2 February, I returned from my work and found that a courier had arrived from Masbate City bearing a letter for me. It came from a Filipino friend who held a high position in the civil government established by the Japanese. The writer had spent the past several weeks in Japanese-held Sorsogon, a small province across the bay on Luzon Island, and had just come to Masbate City by sailboat. The letter read:

> "Before leaving Sorsogon yesterday morning, I had breakfast with several Japanese officers and civilians. They were apparently a group who had been to Masbate before, and some of the civilians have previously lived at Aroroy. They told me that on the morning of 3 February, a large force of Japanese would land at Masbate City and permanently occupy the island. I am passing this information on to you for what it is worth, but I feel sure it is the truth and would advise any Americans who wish to, to leave as soon as possible. They did, however, say that the Americans would not be molested or moved away. Please destroy this letter."

We discussed this information in great detail. The majority believed this to be only another rumor, but even if it was the truth, the Japanese hadn't bothered us before. The letter said they wouldn't molest us this time. So, of the fifteen or so people still in camp, all decided to remain except three: Ken Hansen, Lester Mason, and me. Enough, we thought, was enough; thanks.

Into Lester Mason's small sedan we rapidly loaded everything we thought we could carry. Hansen packed a box containing his little black bag and several personal items that his houseboy had been able to recover from the looters. This he hoped to be able to stash with some Filipino family.

We left soon after midnight, heading for the ranch house of a Spanish-Filipino family we had visited from time to time. There we found only one son and a few servants. The rest of the family, hearing of the probability of a Japanese landing, had moved back into the jungle three kilometers away.

The son took Hansen's box. "I will hide it where it will never be found," he said. "When the war is over, you come back and find me and I will give it to you."

He hid Lester's car in a safe place and guided us to the buck-wheation where the family was hiding. There we were treated to a wonderful breakfast of eggs, rice cakes, meat and *real* milk, and were invited to stay with them until we found out something of the Japanese movements. We knew that should the Japanese find our Filipino friends hiding three Americans they would be severely punished. So we moved to a place about a half-mile away and set up camp.

Located in a small grove with a nearby stream and open fields on three sides, we felt relatively safe from surprise. We built a small lean-to and slung several pieces of heavy canvas between trees for hammocks. Although the curve of them made for lame backs in the morning, we were fairly comfortable. We hoped to be self-sufficient in our makeshift camp, although in reality we knew we would find a reason to visit our nearby friends almost daily; the food would be much better.

On the second day, some of the ranch employees brought word that the Japanese had landed in Masbate City as scheduled and had proceeded to the mine in force. For two more days, we waited. When the next report said that the Japanese were moving into permanent quarters and apparently intended to stay, we decided to go across the Sibuyan Sea to Panay, if transportation could be arranged.

Early the following morning, our friend sent one of his men to a nearby coastal town about ten kilometers away. In the afternoon the man returned with two *cargadores*, porters, to help carry our gear. The man who had recruited the porters served as our guide until we reached the coast. He had also arranged for a boat to take us to Panay.

It was dark before we finally got packed, bid our friends good-bye, and started on the long trail. It was firm and level, and we made good time. Yet the packs grew heavier and heavier, and we were glad when we came to the house of a relative of our Filipino friend. Here, the guide borrowed two horses that we converted into pack animals. At about two o'clock in the morning, we reached the seacoast, unloaded the horses, and dropped everything, including ourselves, onto the sand.

In the moonlight, I looked up and down the beach, trying to spot the boat in which we would sail across open ocean to Panay. I reasoned that an adequate vessel would be rather large and certainly visible. I could see nothing. Soon, silently, three men came from a nearby house. They walked into a grove of palm trees just off the beach, picked up a small boat, and carried it to the water. The boat was about sixteen feet long and not more than eighteen inches wide, with outriggers on both sides. They then went back, got the mast, stood and braced it on the boat, came up to where we were huddled on the sand, and said they were ready to go.

I couldn't believe this boat would hold six people and our baggage. To cross seventy-five miles of ocean in this overgrown canoe seemed impossible. Against our better judgement, our guide managed to convince us that the boat was large enough.

Aside to Ken I said, "That's easy for him to say. He isn't going with us."

There was room, just, for bodies and baggage, but only because two of the crew rode standing on the edge of the boat or on small catwalks leading to the outriggers. Later, we learned that these two men were a very necessary part of the crew. In heavy winds, or even with large swells, the two outrigger men were continuously running back and forth from outrigger to boat, sometimes on one side and sometimes on the other—ballast to keep the craft from overturning. They were often standing on an outrigger in water almost to their hips, only to be three feet above the water in an instant.

For several hours, we sailed along the Masbate coast, always very near shore. Soon after dawn we landed on Jintotolo, a small, beautiful island. Scarcely a mile in diameter, it formed almost a perfect circle and had wide, white sand beaches and was surrounded by coral reefs. The entire island was planted with coconut trees, laid out in symmetrical rows. On the west side stood a large lighthouse and the caretaker's home, both built of stone.

We stayed on Jintotolo only long enough to eat, and were soon on our way once more. While on this picturesque isle, we were fascinated to see several small boats that were under construction. The hulls consisted of an inner and outer skin of tightly woven bamboo. The space between the skins, one or two inches, was filled with a plastic paste made of ground sea shells and some other materials unknown to me. After drying and curing, I was told, the paste becomes very hard, and the boat is then ready for use. Who says concrete ships are new?

Although we were becalmed for an hour or two, our trip was uneventful, if one can call feeling like sitting ducks on a sea without a speck of land in sight "uneventful." At six in the evening, we arrived in Capiz, now named Roxas City, population twenty thousand, on Panay's north coast.

A ride up the sluggish Capiz River took us to a small bamboo dock. We were immediately surrounded by Filipinos, all anxious to see the new Americanos. They told us of several Americans living a short distance away at the Riverside Hotel. Shouldering our packs, with several of the natives sharing our burdens, we soon arrived at the hotel.

A large wooden building with a galvanized iron roof, the Riverside Hotel was not unlike many other buildings in the town. The guest facilities were on the second floor. The ground floor was unfinished and used as a store house and sleeping quarters for the servants (and for an assemblage of animals). Inside we were greeted by many of our friends from Masbate who had arrived previously: the Dakins, the Clardys and their two children, Claude and LaVerne Fertig, and several others.

Claude had been the superintendent of the Capsay mine, between Masbate mine and IXL. A reserve U.S. Army major, he had been called to active duty before hostilities began and had missed all of the adventures and misadventures we had had on Masbate. Here, he was in charge of all engineering work on Panay.

It was 10 February 1942.

five

PANAY

A single-engine Grumman flying boat later joined the fleet. Navy men had retrieved it from almost total submersion off Bataan, replaced the engine with one from a plane previously junked, and restored the rest with salvaged parts from other wrecks. It lacked a tail wheel and most of the fabric under the tail was scraped off.

For two weeks we spent most of our time at Capiz, with occasional short trips to Iloilo on the south coast of the island. Life was slow and easy. We were away from the stress that had been our daily regimen on Masbate. I appreciated being on an island where there was a semblance of a military force on my side of the confrontation.

The food was interesting and varied, and the daily fare of Filipino cuisine did not become boring. Actually this was not really the native diet, for the cooks had been trained by Americans and the meals were as stateside as the cooks' educations and the available supplies could make them.

More evacuees from Masbate arrived around the middle of February. These were some of the people who had opted, several weeks previously, to believe the Japanese's promise that they would not be molested—the gamble Hanson, Mason, and I had not taken. The Japanese had reneged on that promise, one of the early indications that the Japanese word was not worth much.

The new arrivals included Harold and Louise Spencer, Homer

Mann, Graham Nelson, Fred Fredericks, Bob Armstrong, Rose Preiser, Henry and Laura Schuring and Clifford, their son, Jack Treat, and a few others. Graham Nelson recounted their story.

"About forty Japs came to the mine on the afternoon of 3 February and set up camp at the airfield. They called us all together and told us no one would be molested, but we were to stay close to the barracks and the staff house area. It was sort of an internment without being fenced in.

"The Japs visited with us occasionally and were quite friendly. They even brought us some food a few times. But soon a Filipino who had been spying on the Japs for us and feeding us bits of information came with bad news. He had been told by a Japanese officer that the following morning we were to be herded up like cattle, moved to Aroroy, and loaded on a boat to be taken to a concentration camp near Legaspi, on Luzon Island. Our spy said the officer seemed to want this news leaked to us so that there wouldn't be many of us left to move.

"Everybody took off for the hills that evening or early the next morning except Barney Faust and his wife, the Rowes, Harry and Mrs. Morrison and their year-old son, and me. I stayed because I couldn't make up my mind where to go. I hung around the staff house until almost nine o'clock, then got my gear together to move out.

"As I went out the front door I saw a party of Jap soldiers coming up the road. I turned and ran out the back door, crawled under the end porch, and lay there for hours watching the legs of the Japanese as they moved the remaining Americans to trucks. They took them to the boat— and eventually to a concentration camp, I guess.

"In the afternoon I took off, and here I am."

We were now without income-producing jobs, and most of us had no stash of cash, so we sought jobs with the army. I was assigned as Assistant Superintendent of Construction at the Santa Barbara Airfield. Ken Hansen was my boss.

The Santa Barbara Airfield, fifteen miles north of Iloilo on the main road to Capiz, was one of five airfields being constructed under the supervision of mining men from Masbate. Our job was to supervise the earthwork and paving for a landing strip five thousand feet long by three hundred feet wide.

The airfield site was a large, almost level field previously devoted to growing rice. The field was divided into rice paddies—squares about one hundred feet, surrounded by low dirt dikes. Connecting the dikes were shallow, narrow ditches forming a grid to carry irrigation water throughout the field. The water level inside the paddies was carefully controlled during the growing season, for the plants required flooded conditions at certain stages of growth and almost arid conditions at other stages. The farmers used hand pumps, usually made of bamboo, to move the water between the dikes and the ditches to flood or to drain the paddies. Viewed from the air, the paddies formed an enormous checkerboard with all the squares the same color.

Working mainly with hand tools, two thousand men leveled the dikes and low ridges to form an even surface for the paving. To haul dirt from place to place, two men would shovel about a wheelbarrow-load of dirt onto a woven bamboo mat with a long bamboo pole fastened to one edge. They would then pull the other edge of the mat across the load and fasten it to the pole to create a dirt-filled sling. Bearing the ends of the pole on their shoulders, they would tote the dirt to the dumping spot, often at a distance of a hundred yards.

After the dirt base was completed, coral was hauled in by trucks and dumped along the length of the runway. Fist-sized chunks of the coral were placed by hand to form the paved surface, with smaller, walnut-sized pieces stuffed into the crevices. Finally, a thin layer of coral dust was spread on top, well sprinkled with water, and the whole compressed with large rollers pulled by hand.

We constructed a dormitory, complete with bamboo bunks, for soon-to-arrive air corps men. In the surrounding mango groves and bamboo clumps we built some twenty revetments—dikes of earth about eight feet high, roughly following the outlines of the noses and wings of the expected occupants. Palm fronds and cogon grass bales were stored nearby to be placed over the airplanes to hide them. Taxi strips leading to the revetments were left rough and were covered with straw that was raked after being traveled. The camouflage was frequently inspected from the air and the pilots said that even knowing the exact location, it was very difficult to see the revetments and the planes. But how do you camouflage a runway? We didn't.

We made plans to build several dummy planes and scatter them about some distance from the taxiways, hoping they would draw attention from the runway. At our "airplane factory" some one hundred people, mostly girls, were employed in the construction of a dummy P-40 airplane, the prototype of a proposed fake air squadron. A full-sized frame was built of bamboo, tied together with rattan. This framework was covered with abaca cloth, then painted in military aircraft colors. Only one of these mock-ups was completed. It was never used. A good idea for naught.

The Japanese occupation came before the hard surfacing of the entire airstrip was completed, but for two months the dirt field was home base for the "Bamboo Fleet," which operated between this field and Bataan. Little known and completely ignored in history, these pilots are among the bravest, most heroic men I have ever known. I do not remember their names, except for two—Randolph and Bradford. I don't even know if those were first or last names.

The Bamboo Fleet originally consisted of three single-engine aircraft: a two-place Belanca, a four-place Beechcraft, and a four-place Stinson biplane that had been used as a basic trainer by the Philippine air force. The last had two .30-caliber machine guns mounted on its wings. They were later removed and set up on the ground for airfield defense.

A single-engine Grumman flying boat later joined the fleet. Navy men had retrieved it from almost total submersion off Bataan, replaced the engine with one from a plane previously junked, and restored the rest with salvaged parts from other wrecks. It lacked a tail wheel and most of the fabric under the tail was scraped off.

For almost two months, these unarmed planes flew nightly missions to Bataan. They took in food and medicine, mostly malaria-fighting quinine flown up from Australia in B-17's, and brought out mail and a few personnel: one newspaper man; a few high-ranking officers; and one intelligence officer of Japanese ancestry are all I recall, and none of them can I name. Some flights were also made during daylight hours. Bradford told me that his maximum altitude on these flights was twenty feet above the waves.

The last run was made to Corregidor after Bataan had fallen. A round trip, something seldom attempted, was necessary. Two planes left Santa Barbara Airfield soon after dark, expecting to return before daylight. Bradford piloted the Belanca; the Stinson was under the hands of a Philippine Air Lines civilian pilot. It was almost nine in the morning before they returned, and Bradford related the story. "The Corregidor airfield is a very short field we'd never seen before, and we both had minor crackups. I nosed over and made a mess of the metal prop. The Stinson went in with a wing low, broke some struts and scraped most of the fabric off the underside. The guys up there removed and reshaped my prop on an anvil by hand. They patched up the Stinson with adhesive tape and replaced the struts with heavy wire."

Three evacuees returned in the two-place Belanca and five in the four-place Stinson. These eight men were immediately flown to Australia in a B-25, flown by "Pappy" Gunn, a former Philippine Air Lines pilot who was later to be one of the best known pilots in the South Pacific. Pappy had flown to Australia some time previously in a twin-engine Beechcraft, and while returning with a Lockheed Lodestar to augment the Bamboo Fleet, had been shot down in southern Mindanao. He island-hopped to Panay, flew one of the Bamboo Fleet's aircraft to Australia, and returned with the B-25.

Japanese planes flew over almost every day, but they never bothered the Santa Barbara field. They did strafe one of the other fields. Apparently the Japanese knew it was only a question of time before they would occupy Panay, and all the construction work we had done would be just so much "gravy" for them.

During March and April we awaited the arrival of several promised P-40 planes and pilots. Barracks were completed and storage areas prepared, but only two P-40's were ever based there, and those for only a short time. One of them made a belly landing while returning from its first flight. The pilot survived, but the plane was destroyed.

The other P-40, piloted by a Lieutenant Putnam, made one reconnaissance flight over Manila. On his return he reported a concentration of Japanese ships outside the Cebu harbor. We refueled his plane, loaded all the ammo it could carry, and Putnam took off on a lone strafing mission. He was gone about two hours and on his return he said he had strafed several Japanese landing barges without answering fire except from rifles, until Japanese planes arrived and drove him away.

This was the last offensive action taken by the mighty "Panay Air Force." Rumors of an impending Japanese landing became a daily occurrence and the planes left, probably for Mindanao.

Reports from Cebu indicated that the Japanese occupation had been completed there. Japanese warships were reported off the west coast of Panay. With occupation of Panay imminent, we were ordered to stop work on all airfields and prepare for evacuation to the hills.

Ever since the war started, several of us had looked to evacuating to Mindanao Island and sailing from there to Australia if the conflict escalated. Now this seemed to be the next logical step. The captain of an English tanker that had been in the Iloilo harbor since late December had decided to move his ship farther south to what he considered to be greater safety. We signed on as crew to get transportation to Mindanao. However, the captain decided not to risk being sunk on the open seas and scuttled the ship to block the harbor. This left us with no alternative but to seek out a southbound native boat.

Early in the afternoon of a sunny April day, Charlie Smith, Chick Smith, and I, with our few belongings, boarded a *larcha,* a large two-masted sailboat with two outriggers, and left for Guimaras Island. This boat was far larger than any native sailboat I had ever seen—not at all like the "splinter" that had carried us from Masbate to Panay.

About sundown, we anchored in a small bay at the southeast tip of Guimaras to await the sunrise, for the crew refused to sail after dark. The night was filled with the noises of ships passing in the distance. Twice, planes flew directly over us, very low, and turned their landing lights on us for a closer look. We evidently looked harmless, for they didn't bother us. We later learned that the Japanese had landed at Iloilo while we were patiently waiting for daylight here on Guimaras.

Early in the morning we again set sail, arriving at Pontevedra, on the west coast of Negros, in mid-afternoon. After spending a very comfortable night in the company of several American army officers who were stationed there, we left in a small truck for a barrio some twenty miles south, where the road ended. There we again took passage in a small but adequate sailboat, arriving at Tolong Viejo about noon of the following day.

Tolong Viejo was the northern terminus of a provincial highway, the center of a rice growing area, and the location of the headquarters of a detachment of Philippine army troops. As we stepped ashore, we saw a truck loaded with rice that was about to leave. We hitched a ride, and lay atop the rice sacks for about twenty miles to the beach at Zamboanguita. Within thirty minutes we negotiated a ride on a medium sized sailboat to Mindanao. It was then about three o'clock in the afternoon. Had we been traveling on a tour set up by a travel agent, we couldn't have made better time in our move from Santa Barbara to Zamboanguita.

As we were about to shove off, a native ran up the beach shouting, "Wait! Wait! An Americano is coming to see you."

We looked and saw Graham Nelson coming around a point of rock a short distance away. Charlie Smith and I walked along the beach to meet him. After the routine of backslapping and handshaking was done, we spent the next several minutes relating the stories of our adventures to each other. The army had transferred Graham from Panay to Cebu. After the Japanese landing at Cebu, he had crossed over to Negros with Bob Armstrong and another American. They were now on the move to Mindanao. Their small boat was only a few hundred yards down the beach, and they, too, were ready to set sail.

"We've got a smaller and faster boat than yours," he said. "Since the natives tell us there's quite a few Jap ships passing back and forth in the channel, we've decided to wait until dark, when it is safer."

We told him we were all set to leave and thought we would move out now. Then we headed for our boats. A racing challenge was set with his words, "We'll beat you to Dapitan anyway."

Until sundown, about two hours later, the trip was very pleasant. Soon after dark, the wind came up and the seas got rougher and rougher. At around nine o'clock, we encountered gale force winds. Three crew members were riding the outriggers, drenched to the skin, and often standing on an outrigger in water up to the waist. Almost every wave was breaking over the boat. We bailed frantically. The temperature may have been in the high seventies, but because of the rain and the wind, we were freezing in our soaked light shirts. I remember the trip as one of the coldest and most uncomfortable I have ever taken.

Until ten o'clock I was interested in nothing except keeping the boat bailed out, wondering if we were about to overturn, and trying to keep warm. Then we saw lights about two miles dead astern. At first there were only a few small lights, but then a large searchlight started to sweep the water behind us, in front of us, and on both sides. Once or twice it rapidly swept directly over us without stopping. We knew it had to be a Japanese ship. There was absolutely nothing we could do except hope, and maybe pray a little, that the beam of light would not stop directly on us. If that should happen, we would have "bought the farm." It seemed to sweep the sea for hours, although it probably was less than five minutes. When we finally saw it no more, we resumed bailing, certain that luck was still with us.

The storm continued, but took on less significance after that experience.

SIX

MINDANAO

There, we heard a very disquieting story. The crew of a native boat had arrived that morning and told of being intercepted by a Japanese cruiser while crossing the Bohol Sea from Zamboanguita. Their passengers, three Americans and one Chinese, were taken prisoner by the Japanese.

Our landing on Mindanao was not skillfully executed. It was the darkest of nights and we sailed directly into a large fish trap in the shallow waters of Dapitan Bay. We spent over an hour poling the boat this way and that before finding our way through the maze.

In the Philippines, fish traps are found at nearly all beach barrios. Fences of one-inch-wide bamboo strips spaced about an inch apart and laced together with rattan extend for hundreds of yards, forming a large "vee." Anchored into the sandy bottom with the open end facing the deep water, the fences gradually approach each other, funneling toward the narrow entrance to the main body of the trap. The fish pass through the entrance without difficulty, but long bamboo slivers, all pointing inward, keep the fish from exiting through this opening. All day long fishermen, in *barotos,* paddle around inside the traps, harvesting the fish by scooping them into their boats. It is not unusual to find ten or more traps at the entrance to any large river. Even in the bright light of day they present difficulties to incoming sailboats, for the tops of the fences barely break the surface of the water at high tide.

The "bamboo telegraph" had announced our impending arrival, and as we beached the boat, the mayor of Dapitan was on shore to greet us, even though it was now around three in the morning. He led us to his home, where we were fed and bedded. Graham Nelson and his traveling companions hadn't arrived yet, so we retired, confident that we would claim our sailing victory in the morning.

When morning came, Nelson and his companions still hadn't arrived at Dapitan. We waited until noon before considering that Graham's boat may have missed Dapitan and landed instead at Dipolog, some ten miles away. We then set out by bus to look for them, arriving in Dipolog at about three in the afternoon.

There, we heard a very disquieting story. The crew of a native boat had arrived that morning and told of being intercepted by a Japanese cruiser while crossing the Bohol Sea from Zamboanguita. Their passengers, three Americans and one Chinese, were taken prisoner by the Japanese. There was no doubt that the captives were Graham Nelson and his companions. They had waited for the cover of darkness—certainly a more prudent plan than ours. But they had been picked up by the Japanese while we, setting out in broad daylight, had made the crossing safely. We then began to realize how *little* thought and preparation counted, and that plain old luck was what counted most. We would continue to see luck play a large part in our lives.

Regularly scheduled buses were still running in this area of Mindanao, for the Japanese had not yet moved in. The following morning we boarded one to Misamis to establish ourselves once more with the U.S. Army. The bus was overloaded, with passengers riding on the running boards and on the top. The trip was very interesting, for it afforded us a fleeting glimpse of a facet of Filipino life we had not seen before.

Just as the language dialects varied from island to island, so did the industries, the farming methods, and the crops. The Panay farmers' main crops were rice and sugar cane. The farms we saw along this road were very different. While Mindanao's farmers, too, grew rice in abundance, we saw here cultivated coconut groves and banana, pineapple, and cacao plantations—crops with which we were unfamiliar. All the farms and towns and barrios we passed through appeared to be prosperous, and there was no indication of a rapidly approaching war.

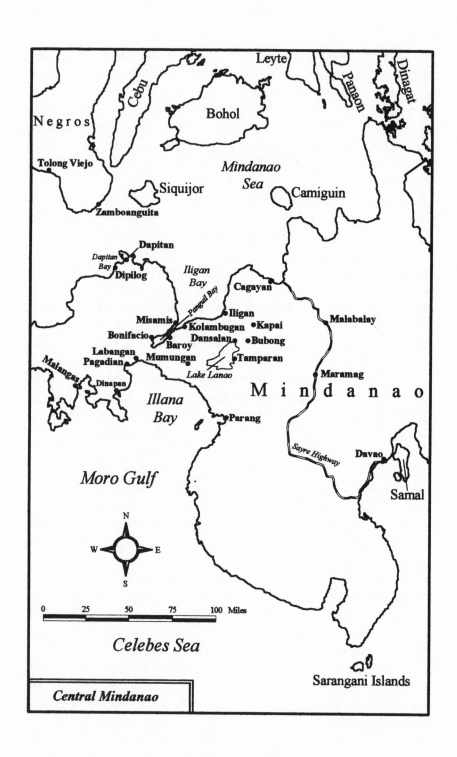

Central Mindanao

At the city of Misamis, we were driven directly to the ferry landing. We boarded the boat and crossed the narrow neck of Iligan Bay to Kolambugan, a lumbering center across the bay. There, an American officer bound for Iligan in a private car offered to take us with him, an offer that we gladly accepted.

The road to Iligan was unpaved, but in fair condition. It wound through many small barrios as it made its way along the coast of Iligan Bay, crossing several shallow rivers, some wide and others narrow, on one-lane wooden bridges. At one of these crossings there was a PT boat beached in the shallow water. Many men, both Americans and Filipinos, were working around it. We were told that the engines were being removed to be taken to Lake Lanao. Soon the hull would be towed there, the engines reinstalled, and the boat would provide transportation for the military around the lake.

We arrived at Iligan at about noon and headed for the one place hospitality was certain to be found in any town—the Catholic convent. Lunch was just being served to the several American officers billeted there, and we were invited to join them.

After a good meal, the conversation turned to the military situation and our proposed trip to Australia. Without exception, the officers and priests advised against trying to sail to Australia at this time of the year. The northeast monsoon, on which we would be dependent, blows almost continuously from November to May, but it was now being replaced by the southwest winds.

"You ain't got a chance of making it," they insisted. "Not 'til November or December."

Although we were determined to attempt the trip, we finally decided to follow their advice and delay our departure. Meanwhile, we would pitch our lot with this remnant of the army until later in the year.

At the time the military situation on Mindanao was rather confusing. The main body of troops, both American and Filipino, was scattered along the Sayre Highway, the one central artery stretching from Cagayan to Davao, with headquarters in Malaybalay. These troops were under the leadership of Maj. Gen. William Sharp, commander of all the Mindanao forces. The several existing airfields were located along this route. The few B-17's still flying to and from Australia landed near Malaybalay.

With headquarters near Dansalan, on Lake Lanao, was a second force under the command of Brig. Gen. Guy O. Fort, a former U.S. Army officer who had served as commanding officer of the Philippine Constabulary in Mindanao since his retirement many years before. General Fort had been enforcing American and Philippine laws among the Moros and was an expert in handling these warlike people. Except for a few American officers, both of these forces were made up of Filipinos, mostly Christians, although the training of Moros for possible future guerrilla duty was well under way.

Besides these two forces, there were many small, scattered groups of navy and air force personnel who had long since lost any connection with their ships or their military units. They had attached themselves to these army units as a means of survival, and were assigned to specific army duties although they were not directly under the command of any army force. These scattered groups eventually formed the nuclei of many of the guerrilla organizations.

Transportation to Dansalan being easily arranged, we left early in the afternoon by army truck. After leaving the lowlands along the coast, the vehicle ground its way up a steep, tortuous road through deep forest. Occasionally we passed through a small, level valley with a several-house barrio in the center. Much of the road closely paralleled the Argus River, which flows from Lake Lanao northward to the sea. Dropping nearly five thousand feet in about five miles, the Argus has a potential hydroelectric capacity exceeded by no other river in the Philippines, although at the time it was underdeveloped.

Dansalan was a small city—population two thousand or so—located on the shore of Lake Lanao. It was a popular resort town because of its relatively cool climate, few mosquitoes, and, therefore, absence of malaria. There were several fancy—by local standards—resort hotels operated by Americans. Almost all the native inhabitants were Moros, and their habits and customs were of great interest to us, as we had never before seen a Moro village.

Filipinos could be divided into three major religious groups: Mohammedan, Christian, and "other." The Moros, or Mohammedans, occupied much of Mindanao, especially the mountainous western area and the Zamboanga Peninsula. Christian Filipinos, mostly Roman Catholics, made up almost ninety percent of the total Philippine population. They lived mainly on the islands north of Mindanao, although in recent years they had been moving to Mindanao in increasing numbers, until they now made up over fifty percent of the population of that island. The "others"—Minobos, Igorots, Magahats, and other semi-civilized groups—were scattered throughout the islands.

The Moros were rugged individualists. They were proud of themselves, their religion, and their habits. They had no desire to copy American customs. The wealthiest Moro may have owned an automobile or a watch and would smoke an American cigarette when offered to him. But his greatest pride came with the ownership of a modern rifle or shotgun, meant only to simplify his way of life, not to change it. Many of the younger Moros spoke fair to good English since it was taught in the schools. It was frequently spoken in their homes as well.

For centuries the Catholics, under Spanish rule, had lived by the tenets of, and under the control of, the Roman church. Under the protective arm of America for the past forty years, a trend toward a Western type of civilization had gradually emerged. This created some conflicts with the teachings of the church—mainly economic—for the people began to spend more of their meager earnings on themselves and donated less to the Church. They purchased cars, radios, American-style clothes, electric refrigerators, and, in general, tried to follow American habits and customs. Not that they were completely successful in becoming Americanized, but even the poorest *tao* hoped to someday be able to buy American products.

The "others" were pagans, each group with its own brand of worship of a deity. Many shunned civilization as we know it. Some Igorot tribes, for example, lived in the jungles where they survived by killing animals with their skill with a bow and arrow, frequently eating them without cooking, and often slept at night nestled in a pile of leaves.

We stayed at a hotel owned by an American couple. It was quite modern, operated on the American plan, and the meals were largely of imported food. It was filled with American and English refugees like us. A few army officers also stayed there.

After we spent two days wandering through the town, discussing the military situation and the impending Japanese occupation, we were given assignments with the army and departed to our various posts. Charlie Smith was sent back to Iligan to make preparations for blowing up the concrete dock should the evacuation of that town become necessary. Chick Smith, who had been the chief mechanical engineer at the Masbate mines, went to a motor pool on the west side of the lake, about ten miles away, to take charge of automotive repairs. I was sent to General Fort's headquarters at Bubong, about fifteen miles southeast, to take charge of road and bridge construction.

Bubong was a small Moro barrio located in the flat Lake Lanao basin at the edge of the jungle-covered mountains that rose abruptly out of the plains. About one mile back into the jungle stood our headquarters, and a dark and dreary place it was. A few semipermanent buildings had been built of bamboo and rattan for use as bodegas. A few temporary barracks built of the same materials had been constructed, well scattered under the trees. The rainy season had just begun and the camp rapidly became a quagmire. The roads, those in the mountains as well as those on the plains, became more impassable with each day. It was my job to grade, ditch, and hard-surface these roads. I was thankful that most of the grading and ditching was completed before I arrived.

All the work was done by hand under what, at times, proved to be extremely trying conditions. Small gangs of Moro laborers were assigned to sections of the road. Rocks three to six inches in size were hauled in and, like the coral paving of the airports on Panay, laid on the roadbed by hand. Some twenty to thirty gangs were employed, each with a Moro capataz in charge. Without Hassan, the foreman, I could have done nothing, for only he could get the gangs to work toward a common end. Each gang was a separate entity under direct control of its capataz, who was usually chief of the small tribe from which the whole crew came. Men could never be transferred from one group to another, and certain groups could not even be assigned to work near certain other groups. Knives were carried by everyone as a part of their working garb, and the possibility of the knives being used in hand-to-hand combat with an adjoining group was ever-present.

Hassan went everywhere with me. He spoke English quite well and served as my guide and as my interpreter, passing my instructions to the teams. He also was my instructor in Moro habits and customs.

A major problem was finding more laborers, for the hard-surfacing work would soon be impossible because of the intensity of the rains. The only way to hire laborers was to find a *datu*—a Moro chieftain—who had enough relatives or friends to make up a full gang. We rapidly ran out of sources.

One afternoon, Hassan and I visited Sultan Sa Romaine at his home. We were cordially received and were supplied with several more gangs. Sultan Sa Romaine was the leader, both politically and religiously, of all the Maranao Moros. He was liked and respected by both Moros and Americans.

His son, Aleonto, had recently graduated from the University of the Philippines, and we had long discussions of the war situation. We agreed that the Japanese occupation would soon come and that they would probably occupy the settled portions of the island without great difficulty. However, we were also sure that guerrilla action would continue under General Fort indefinitely. He assured me that the Moros would never surrender and would assist the Americans in their guerrilla fighting.

I didn't feel comfortable in trusting Aleonto. He was frightful-looking, having a hollowed-out depression where the eye he lost in a brawl had been, and he wore a permanent snarl on his face. But I misjudged him, for he became one of the strongest resistance leaders among the Maranao Moros. Frankly, I never trusted Hassan entirely, either. It is hard to trust someone you have known for only a short time, especially if his coal-black teeth are filed to points and a *kris* is strapped to his waist. But he was a good companion and helper. We had few disagreements.

Once I thought he wasn't cooperative. It was our second morning together. We were standing in the middle of the road discussing the operations and I thought a couple of changes should be made.

"Hassan," I said, "Have this ditch dug a little deeper."

"Why, Sir," he answered.

"Because it is not big enough to carry the water. And also widen the road a little here for a turnout."

"Why, Sir," he answered again.

I was a bit peeved by his responses, but said nothing to him. However, at noon I remarked to Lt. John D. Stuckenberg, engineering officer for General Fort, that Hassan didn't follow instructions too well, for he kept questioning my orders.

"Every time I tell him to have the workmen do something differently, he asks 'Why?'"

The lieutenant and several other officers at the lunch table laughed, then explained Hassan's continued query. "Why," pronounced "wy-ee," is the Moro dialect word for "yes."

Road construction didn't continue for long. About 7 May, Japanese troops landed in force at Parang on the south coast, and the following day at Cagayan on the north coast. Dansalan was bombed and most of the city destroyed, fortunately with small loss of life.

A civilian evacuation camp was opened for the Americans and the English at Tamparan and many people were moved there. Many, myself included, remained with the army. Supplies were moved rapidly to the headquarters camp at Bubong. For several days, the roads were crowded. Luckily, there was no rain.

The holding action along the Parang-Dansalan road was not going well and the Japanese forces were reported to be advancing rapidly from the south. The army troops were, of course, under orders to continue to resist, but we civilians were given permission to leave if we desired, although the army would be glad to have us Americans stay to help lead the Moros.

About this time Hassan and I had a serious conversation regarding the proposed guerilla movement. His chief concern was whether or not I expected to stay and fight as a guerrilla. After I had said I was staying, he asked, "Are you married?"

I, of course, answered, "Yes."

"Is your wife American or Christian?"

I hesitated for a second or two before saying, "American." I then explained that my wife and my son were also Christians, but were living in America.

"Mister Ham," he said, "If you are with me in the guerrilla, you will live with me. My people will take care of you. Do not worry."

This however, never came to pass.

On the morning of the Japanese landings, all the Moro crews were still working on the roads. One large crew of Moros had been sent several miles back into the jungle to clear trails and to put a roof on a large building to be used as emergency headquarters should further evacuation become necessary.

Early in the day, we heard rumors of considerable shooting at the jungle camp. At first, the story was that Moros and Filipino soldiers had started shooting at each other. I could see a tense situation developing, and it seemed to me that every Moro laborer along the road was getting ready to turn against the American and Filipino soldiers in retaliation. A Moro uprising on the heels of the Japanese landings could really become a problem. For almost an hour, this tense situation continued. Then we learned that the battle was a personal feud among a few Moros. One man had been killed and several injured. Learning that the trouble was entirely between Moros was quite a relief to me. Hassan and I moved down the road in a small car to another section of the work.

After driving for several miles, checking the construction as we went along, we saw a group of about fifteen people walking toward us—they looked like a parade, occupying the entire width of the roadway. They were waving their arms and shouting.

Hassan said urgently, "Get to the side of the road and stop. Get your gun ready but keep it out of sight. I don't think there will be trouble but I don't know." I did as told and sat there waiting, with no idea of what was going on or what might happen. As the group came close, I could see that an old woman was leading them. She was skinny and wrinkled, stark naked above the waist, displaying the effects of pectoral muscle atrophy. Grasped in her two hands was a three-foot-long sword that she swung from side to side and above her head. All the rest were Moro men. They were also naked above the waist and were armed with swords, knives, and guns.

As they marched down the road, a continuous chant or wail came from their lips as they all brandished their arms from side to side. They passed by us without looking to right or left, rousing in me a great sigh of relief. Hassan then explained that they were all relatives of the Moro who had been killed that morning. The leader was the mother of the slain boy and was leading the band to a battle to avenge her son's death. He also told me that the long two-handed sword that she was carrying, which he called a *campilon*, was an heirloom that had probably been in the family for centuries.

Weeks later I was able to examine several of these swords closely. Each was inlaid with Spanish coins bearing dates prior to 1700. Most had intricately carved handles, and the blades were etched with complicated designs. Some were decorated with silver filigree and mother-of-pearl inlays as well. In contrast, the scabbard, or sheath, was crude and unornamented. It was simply two pieces of thin, roughly-shaped wood placed on both sides of the blade and tied together with two or three flimsy strips of rattan. Custom decreed that the blade must never be unsheathed unless blood was let. In use, the long sword was swung with both hands, scabbard and all, at the victim. The razor-sharp blade easily cut through the rattan bindings and continued on into the victim's body. Afterward, a new scabbard was made.

Hassan also explained to me the other knives that were being carried—the kris and the *barong*. The kris is a stabbing knife, usually about eighteen inches long and one and one-half inches wide—razor-sharp on both edges as well as on the fairly blunt point. The blade may have up to seven waves in it, and each knife has a specific native name indicating the number of waves in the blade. The handle is quite ornate and highly decorated with silver and pearls. The barong is a chopping knife, used mostly for beheading. It has a blade also about eighteen inches long but only one edge is sharpened while the other edge is almost one-quarter of an inch thick. At the center, the blade is three inches wide, tapering to a sharp point at the end and back to almost no width at the handle, which is of highly polished hardwood.

An unusual thing about the handles of all Moro knives used as weapons is an attached strip of cheap, colored cotton cloth about two feet long. Before going into battle, the cloth is wound around the palm and fingers of the hand and back over the end of the handle, thus effectively tying the knife to the hand. Unless this is done, it gets so slick with blood that it can't be grasped tightly.

I never did learn whether the party was successful in gaining revenge, but I believe they turned back before encountering the foe.

After the relatives of the slain boy passed, Hassan and I drove about three miles to where a road was being constructed that would run to the site of a new camp. This camp's purpose was meant to be secret. But in the Philippines there were no secrets, and everyone knew that this would be the headquarters for Gen. Jonathan M. "Skinny" Wainwright after the inevitable fall of Corregidor. It was never occupied by him, however, for he was imprisoned by the Japanese when he surrendered the Philippine Islands to the enemy.

While inspecting the road, I was introduced to General Sharp, who complimented me on the way the construction work was being done—then chewed me out for allowing the trucks to become so bunched up as to present a perfect target for Japanese planes. It mattered not, for it was the last day of major roadway construction. In the future, all would be *destruction.*

On the second day after the landings, the hospital was moved from Dansalan to Bubong. Wounded men, mostly Filipinos, started coming in, relating stories of the unstoppable Japanese steamroller they had encountered. Dansalan was bombed and burned, and daily our defending forces dropped back farther. Most of my time was spent near Bubong, as there was much work to be done around headquarters. Supplies were continually going out to the forces or being brought back when they were no longer needed. The rains had started, and every afternoon almost infinitesimal clouds suddenly gathered together and dropped rain by the bucketfuls. To get trucks up the steep, winding dirt road was an arduous task.

About this time, two PBY's—twin-engined amphibious airplanes—had been sent from Lake Lanao to Corregidor to evacuate the nurses and a few key officers. On return, one of the planes landed at Malaybalay to refuel, then proceeded to Australia. The other developed engine trouble and during its landing on Lake Lanao, the hull was punctured. It was necessary to beach the ship. Since repairs were thought to be impossible, all the nurses were sent to Malaybalay by truck, there to be picked up by a B-17 being flown in from Australia. The Japanese, however, captured Malaybalay and no more planes arrived. The nurses were taken prisoner and interned at Santo Tomas University in Manila for the duration of the war.

The stricken PBY was not a total loss, however. Working around the clock for the next two days, stranded army air corps mechanics repaired the jagged holes with abaca cloth and pitch. Whether the patches would hold for a takeoff was very doubtful, but the pilot took on board any *navy* personnel who wished to risk the flight. He refused to take any army men, although there were many who had worked on the ship who begged to be taken along. It took off late in the afternoon, with the advancing Japanese only a few miles away. It was loaded to less than half its capacity, and arrived safely in Australia a short time later.

Although the air corps men who had been left on the shore of the lake were very bitter, most of them eventually realized that the pilot's refusal was not due to any organizational rivalry or animosity. He had been ordered to bring out a specified group—a group now prisoners of the Japanese. The army was still under orders to defend the Philippines. As far as he knew, any army men who left the islands would be deserters. He did not wish to be a party to desertions.

Within a week after the landing at Parang, the Japanese forces were occupying nearly all of the western shore of Lake Lanao. They were rapidly advancing unopposed from the south along the east side of the lake toward Dansalan, for the Filipino troops were deserting en masse, throwing away their arms and uniforms and fading into the civilian population. Colonel Vesey, with what was left of his regiment, had moved back to the camp that had been constructed for General Wainwright. After dark, we were to move this force to our camp near Bubong.

Lieutenant Stuckenberg and I left Bubong in the afternoon with the few trucks that were still operational and located the remains of Vesey's regiment. For the past week they had been fighting a very fine holding action against overwhelming odds along the west shore of the lake, and even now were being pulled back only because the encircling action of the Japanese had almost cut off their last chance of withdrawal.

Colonel Vesey was asleep on the ground when I first saw him. With the exception of the guards and sentries, the entire regiment— officers and enlisted men, Americans and Filipinos—lay amid the trees, all resting or sleeping. This was their first opportunity to enjoy the luxury of rest in almost a week. For a long hour, "Stukey" and I waited, talking to some of Vesey's officers who were awake, biding our time until four o'clock, when the colonel had left orders to be awakened.

At one minute after four, the entire camp was a mass of activity, preparing for the trip to Bubong. It was then I had my introduction to Col. Robert H. Vesey. He was a small man, and very calm. Nothing seemed to bother him. News, favorable or unfavorable, made no visible impression on him. A career officer, a graduate of West Point, he instilled confidence by his demeanor. The only unmilitary thing about him was the small monkey that sat on his shoulder most of the time.

I don't believe I ever saw the monkey more than ten feet away from him—most often, it was in his lap.

Until five o'clock, we lolled under the trees, opining on the future while awaiting chow call. It was now only a matter of days before the Japanese would control all roads. We were sure that organized guerrilla action would continue indefinitely. Colonel Vesey asked me if I expected to go with the civilians to their evacuation camp. When I told him that I would prefer to remain with the army, he was quite pleased. He said he thought it was a wise choice, and probably safer than going with the civilians. He then asked if I would take charge of the loading and transportation of the troops, which I was glad to do.

Immediately after eating, we loaded the trucks with most of the equipment and the first contingent of troops. Though the men jammed every conceivable space, we were only able to get about half of them on the trucks. They left at about six-thirty with two Americans and most of the Filipino officers. The rest of us settled down to await the return of the trucks for a second load, expected to be at about nine o'clock.

All was calm. The moon was full. Our conversation had little to do with the war until about eight o'clock, when the silence was broken by a fusillade of rifle shots, which continued spasmodically for some time. They were far in the distance and seemed to come from the Bubong area. It appeared almost certain that the Japanese had moved faster than expected and had ambushed our truck convoy.

Colonel Vesey immediately moved all of us away from the road and into the trees, then set out guards in all directions. He sent a small party of Filipinos on back trails toward Bubong with orders to return with information as soon as possible. The rest of us could do nothing but wait. All was silent, but we started hearing things—inexplicable noises that never developed into anything. Again we relaxed, albeit tensely, and settled back.

It was nearly eleven before the lights of several vehicles could be seen coming down the road. The same old question arose: Were they our trucks returning or was it a Japanese convoy? Several of us hid in the ditch along the road. Soon they were before us, and we recognized our own equipment and drivers.

The rifle fire? Someone had failed to advise the Bubong guards of the impending arrival of the convoy. The guards, believing that a

Japanese column was approaching, opened fire. The troops in the convoy, assuming that Bubong had been taken by the Japanese, leaped from the trucks, took cover, and returned the fire. It was almost fifteen minutes before the situation cleared. By that time many of the troops seeking cover had scattered, and it took almost two hours to get them reassembled, reloaded, and taken on to the camp. Three or four men were killed and several were wounded due to this brief and inexcusable mistake.

The rest of us loaded onto the returned trucks as rapidly as possible and arrived in Bubong about an hour later.

Confusion reigned at the Bubong camp for the next week. We lacked a G-2 section to assemble and interpret intelligence information. For example, a large column of Japanese troops was reported to have passed along the east shore of Lake Lanao toward Dansalan at about nine in the morning following our arrival at Bubong, but this information was never confirmed. The information had come from some Moro scouts and from a few Americans who dared to make nightly trips to the lake. But no one would say they *actually saw* them.

It became prudent to move army headquarters farther back into the hills, and to begin guerrilla activities. General Fort and most of his staff moved ten kilometers eastward into the mountains, leaving Colonel Vesey in charge at Bubong. All supplies and movable equipment were moved back into a newly prepared position in the hills.

The headquarters camp was relocated into the heavy jungle, about a mile and a half above the plains. Actually, it comprised two small camps. Halfway up the steep, winding road was the location of most of the Philippine troops and engineers. At the end of the road were located the headquarters, many of the largest warehouses, and the hospital. Between the two camps, the road passed for several hundred yards along a side hill, from which the valley could be seen.

Heavy rain storms were frequent, and the road became impassable on many days. Wounded soldiers were still being brought in almost every day, and there were probably fifty or sixty in the temporary hospital.

Colonel Vesey immediately stationed a lookout at the side hill, with two American officers and a small detachment of Philippine soldiers on guard there at all times. A larger group of Filipinos was deployed along the base of the hill, also as guards.

Vesey's unit had few American officers, so he inducted me into the U.S. Army as 2d lieutenant. The colonel told me that since I had indicated I was planning to stay with the army and help them, it would be advisable for me to wear insignia. On a morning we were all gathered around in camp, he asked the group if anyone had any extra insignia of any kind. The only response was from a naval lieutenant commander. He had some small oak leaves. These the colonel gave to me, with the remark that a promotion from 2d lieutenant to major in thirty seconds was the most rapid advancement in rank he had ever seen.

For the next week, I spent most of my time on lookout duty without seeing any sign of Japanese in the plains below. Nor did I receive any reports of Japanese movements. It was known that there was a large force of Japanese in Dansalan. Apparently, few were moving out into the country. General Fort and his party returned from the upper camp after several days. He took command, making arrangements for guerrilla warfare.

Col. Alejandro Suarez, a Moro-English mestizo who had previously been a major in the Philippine Constabulary, was put in charge of guerrilla training and began organizing the Moros and Philippine soldiers for eventual guerrilla warfare, in anticipation of our impending forced move into the hills. Colonel Suarez was about fifty years old and, at over six feet tall, he was one of the tallest Filipinos I have ever met. He spoke very good English, as well as all Moro and many Philippine dialects.

Rumors of impending Japanese movements were quite common, and we began the transfer of supplies and wounded back even farther into the hills. Several times Japanese planes flew over us at very low altitudes. They did not seem to locate us and there was no shooting.

For several days, General Fort had been trying to make radio contact with General Sharp, who was near Malaybalay. With only one small portable transmitter available, he was not successful. The larger radio equipment had been destroyed during the Japanese advance on us a week previously.

During this period, we set out to destroy all heavy equipment and supplies that could not be moved back into the hills to prevent it from falling into the hands of the Japanese. For several days we were engaged in blowing up bridges, destroying automobiles and tractors, and burning ammunition and gasoline supply dumps.

It was merely a matter of a short time until organized resistance to the Japanese on Mindanao would cease.

seven

INTO THE JUNGLE

We struggled to find enough dry wood under fallen trees to have a small campfire, and roasted a parrot that Smith had shot during the day. His shooting this bird caused a minor rift between us, for I was convinced that the noise of his rifle would draw a horde of Japanese soldiers to us.

Charlie Smith finished destroying the concrete dock at Iligan just as several Japanese freighters rose over the horizon and headed into the bay. A rather large but dilapidated wooden bodega stood on timber piles a short distance from the destroyed dock. It extended about twenty feet past the low water mark toward the bay. An attached short, narrow loading pier reached farther into the bay. It, too, was supported on timber piles. He had not set charges under the bodega or the pier, for they looked like they were about to collapse under their own weight. They certainly would be blown over by the concussion from the concrete dock blast. Explosives were in short supply and there was no need to waste them, he reasoned.

But when the concrete dock split into a thousand pieces, the bodega and the pier merely swayed a bit and remained erect. Smith wanted to move right in and set some charges under the old bodega and pier, for they had to be destroyed as well. But he didn't have time to do that now, for the convoy was steaming rapidly toward the city. He'd have to destroy them later.

Smith loaded the remainder of his blasting supplies into a baroto, then hid it in a cove about two miles away. From there, he hiked to a nearby hillside from which he could see the town and observe the Japanese landing. The four ships of the convoy anchored just off-shore. One by one they moved to the end of the pier, each spewing men and equipment which were quickly moved to shore. Smith, not-ing the size and weight of the vehicles and other equipment being unloaded, realized that the pier was not as decrepit as he had previ-ously judged it to be. He also noted that a major-sized military unit was about to invade and occupy the Iligan Bay area. What he did not know was that this was one of several like units being put ashore simultaneously around the periphery of Mindanao. The occupation had begun.

He continued to observe the Japanese activities for another day, meanwhile preparing his blasting charges well in advance of his next mission. He carefully crimped a blasting cap to one end of a ten-foot length of slow-burning fuse cord, then taped the capped end to a two-hundred-yard length of high-speed fuse cord. At the other end of the high-speed fuse cord he crimped another cap which he taped to a stick of dynamite. He prepared five like charges, hoping he would have time to plant all of them.

Under cover of moonless midnight darkness, Charlie quietly paddled his craft toward his target. The port side outrigger hugged dangerously close to the matted, twisted roots of the mangrove trees lining the shore. To starboard the black sea and blue-black sky blended into nothingness.

The mangrove swamp suddenly ended. As he slid past a few hundred feet of open sandy beach he was exposed to the view of anyone who might be answering a call of nature in the shallow wa-ters. He soon reached the rubble of the destroyed dock, apparently undetected, but even among the rubble he was not completely shielded from view. He maneuvered his dugout around and between the chunks of broken concrete to the wooden pier.

Under the pier he was again hidden from sight. He moved among the pilings to the bodega, being very careful to keep the baroto from bumping against the structure, a noise that would attract unwanted attention. He quietly inserted the five dynamite sticks into several crevices, a task that proved to be so easy that he cursed himself for not having prepared more charges. Then he slowly slipped the baroto out from under the pier, unrolling the fuse cords as he moved back to the cover of the mangrove trees.

"*Now come the fireworks*," he said to himself. He lit the ends of the five slow-burning fuse cords and dropped them overboard. Although underwater, they would continue to burn for about five minutes, giving him time to move farther away from the blast. When the fire reached the first fuse caps they would explode and ignite the fast-burning cord, and in an instant all hell would break loose as five sticks of dynamite went off in rapid succession. Charlie paddled the baroto farther offshore to get a better view of the bodega and to observe his handiwork.

The blast came on schedule. Apparently gasoline and munitions had been stacked in the bodega. Burning chunks of timber flew high into the air and in all directions. Almost immediately the remains of the bodega and many nearby houses burst into flames. Munitions, too, had been scattered far and wide and they exploded sporadically, adding to the bedlam.

"Hot damn!" Charlie shouted. "That got the bastards!"

He then hightailed it to the protective cove, hid the baroto, and hiked to his observation spot. He sat there until dawn, looking down on the town and enjoying the confusion he had created.

Had Charles Smith left Iligan immediately after destroying the concrete dock, he would have had an easy hike along the highway to Lake Lanao and on to Bubong, where I was located. But not even he could believe the speed with which the Japanese occupied that highway. In the extra two days he had taken to destroy the old bodega and pier, they had taken possession of the first five miles of the road toward Lake Lanao, and had slowed their move to the south only to allow the supply lines to catch up with the spearhead. With that route closed to him, Charlie had to make his way through dense jungle instead.

With a young Filipino for a guide, he decided to try to cross the mountains to Mala, in the vicinity of General Sharp's headquarters. This route would keep them clear of the Japanese forces. After three or four days of plodding lost through the jungle, hacking trails where none existed, they stumbled into Bubong, clothing in shreds and soaked with blood from the lesions left by leeches encountered in the many streams they had crossed. This had been Charlie's baptism to the rigors of moving through virgin jungle. I had yet to have this experience, but the description he related told me that traveling through the rugged Mindanao jungle was not a recreational hike in the woods.

Although they were separated by only sixty miles, communications between General Fort and General Sharp were practically nonexistent. Radio contact had disappeared when the troops, in panic, destroyed the equipment to keep it from falling into enemy hands. Dependable couriers were not to be had, for they had sensed the futility of trying to hold off the Japanese and had deserted, discarding their uniforms and arms and blending into the civilian population as nonparticipants in the struggle.

Charlie Smith and I decided to volunteer for courier duty as a one-time assignment. "Volunteer" is a dirty word in the military, but we believed it might be easier to arrange for our trip to Australia from General Sharp's headquarters in the Malaybalay area than from the Lake Lanao area. We had no basis for this belief, for neither point was near the ocean. But unknowingly we had been infected with the "keep moving" bug. Every American, it seemed, felt it was safer to keep on the move rather than stay in one place, a moving target being harder to hit than a sitting duck.

We departed the next day, carrying several sealed courier pouches, with two of General Fort's personal guides to show us the trail for the first day. Then they were to return to General Fort's side, and Charlie and I would have to find new guides—or go it alone.

From the camp at Bubong, the trail for the first few miles was easy to follow, for it was the frequently used route to the upper camp. Beyond that camp the trail became less distinct, and even the guides had trouble following it. We had to backtrack several times when the trails dead-ended. We climbed higher and higher into the mountains to an elevation of five thousand feet or more. At that altitude the jungle was not nearly as thick as at lower elevations, so hiking was comparatively easy, except that in the rarer air one's stamina is reduced.

The trail followed the ridges, but frequently would descend almost a thousand feet to cross a stream. Then we faced a steep climb to another ridge.

There were many orchids growing in the trees above us. Several times our guides asked if we would like to have some, but we saw no reason to carry bouquets. The only women we would want to give them to were half a world away.

The first night we camped in the jungle at a small, almost abandoned barrio. There we were able to hire two cargadores and the next morning we took to the trail again. The guides returned to General Fort. The trail was now considerably more distinct and we had no trouble following it.

In our backpacks we had a goodly supply of hand-rolled cigarettes, loose tobacco, and cigarette papers. But we had very few matches. Since we were heavy smokers, neither Smith nor I would extinguish a cigarette without the other taking a light from it.

Leeches were a constant problem, for we were hiking on swampy trails and through many stagnant ponds. We bound our pant legs tight to our ankles, but we still had to stop every fifteen or twenty minutes to remove the slimy, slithering bastards from our legs.

One of the best ways to remove a leech is to touch it with the hot tip of a cigarette. The leech then withdraws its head from the skin and drops off. Pulling them off or scraping them off with a sharp knife are not wise ideas, for this leaves the problem part—the germ-covered head—embedded in the skin. This is certain to become an infected spot that will grow into a tropical ulcer, which is usually quite painful. The spit from a juicy chaw of tobacco will also make leeches back out and fall off. But no matter what method you use or how careful you are, leeches will invariably leave pretty nasty sores.

When we left Bubong, dress shoes and work boots were only a memory. Now we wore homemade shoes that the Filipinos made in fairly large quantities as a cottage industry. The soles were made of woven and braided Manila hemp; the uppers were made of *ramie* cloth, a rough and fairly durable material made from a flax-like plant. These homemade shoes were fairly satisfactory—certainly much better than being barefooted—but under the very wet and rough trail conditions they disintegrated in two weeks or less. And unlike leather or canvas, they offered no protection from leeches.

On the second day, moving more-or-less to the east, we exited from the uninhabited jungle onto a wide ridge and came upon another barrio. There were quite a few houses and cultivated plots of land, but no people. One house had been burned, the charred timbers still reeking with the stench of burning. We immediately assumed that the Japanese had raided the area, although it was difficult to believe that the Japanese had penetrated this far into the jungle. We continued on the trail, but with increased alertness. Late in the afternoon we descended into a large, well-populated valley. There we learned that a marauding gang of Filipinos had recently raided this settlement as well as the one we had passed through earlier in the day. Here, too, one house had been burned. Other than the two burnings, there was relatively little destruction. Both settlements had been ransacked, although little but foodstuffs had been taken.

The looting had a significant effect upon our well-being. We had carried only sufficient food to last us for two days, intending to buy or beg food each day. We weren't able to obtain anything edible except for a few small pieces of meat given to us by some Philippine army officers.

We camped overnight in an abandoned house. Behind it stood a jackfruit tree that had not been stripped by the marauders. Jackfruit is a form of breadfruit, about the size and shape of a small watermelon, but with a very rough dark-green exterior and large seeds. The fruit grows directly from the trunk of the tree, not from the limbs. Although neither Smith nor I had ever seen one, we had heard that the jackfruit, when cooked, was very good to eat. We did not know that it was important for the fruit to be ripe. These were not.

We picked a large one and attempted to peel it prior to cooking. The fruit was made up of hundreds of segments, each a hard seed about the size of a large almond surrounded by a thin, soft layer of pulpy flesh. Being green, it also contained a very sticky, milk colored juice—so sticky that, after cutting the jackfruit open, we found it impossible to clean the knife or our hands. For the next three or four days our hands were like magnets, clinging to everything we touched. Much later, we learned to coat our hands and tools with coconut oil first to ease the clean up process. We boiled the pulpy flesh for a long time and, although it was not very tasty, it filled the stomach. The seeds, when roasted, tasted a bit like small potatoes and were a very welcome staple.

The Filipino officers who had given us the meat had been members of General Sharp's forces. I say "had been," for General Sharp had surrendered. They had left the General's command and were trying to get to the coast to return by boat to Luzon, their home island. The leader of this little group, a major, told us that with General Sharp's surrender the Japanese now had complete control of the island. The major expected the Americans to return soon and he and his men would then be called upon to fight again. This was not a pleasant thought among some of his troops, who seemed to think it might be better to continue under Japanese domination rather than to go through the horrors of another military operation.

We found it hard to believe that General Sharp had surrendered, so the next morning we continued eastward into the mountainous jungle in search of him. The trails we used were good. We passed many *kaingins,* or farms, in which upland rice, corn, sweet potatoes, also called *camotes,* and casaba grew. *Kaingineros,* nomadic farmers, move into the mountains during the dry season and cut and burn all the vegetation from an area of several acres. They plant their crops, which yield bountifully for about two years until the jungle plants, proliferating at a much faster rate than the domestic crops, reclaim the land. The farmers surrender to the rank growth, abandon the fight, and select a new location. There, the clearing, planting, and surrender cycle is repeated. Few substantial homes are built in these areas, as the families simply camp there for a few months while tending the crops, then return to their villages until the next growing season.

Approximately two weeks had passed since the Japanese landings on Mindanao. Most of these kaingins had already been raided by retreating Filipino and American soldiers and transients, and it was very difficult to find food along the trail. We camped that night at a small settlement, where we were welcomed, although not with the enthusiasm usually attendant to the arrival of Americans in a village. Obtaining food was a problem. We ate the leftovers from the natives' tables, depriving the mangy dogs—themselves only days away from the spit—of the scraps. Here again we were told, but we still refused to believe, that General Sharp had surrendered.

The next morning we continued on the trail. By midday we were clear of the jungle and moved into large, grassy plains on which there were hundreds of cattle grazing. We hiked for several hours through the meadowlands, then came to a small barrio where we encountered two self-important politicians on their way to offer their allegiance and their services to the Japanese, at that time less than ten miles away. They told us that all of this district was now occupied by the Japanese—"very kind people," they said—and they insisted that we surrender to the Japanese. When we indicated that we did not intend to surrender they ordered us out of the town and refused us food. However, as we were leaving, one townsman told us that he would advise us not to surrender. He then told one of his sons to follow us and give us some dried meat and other foods when we were out of sight.

Now convinced that General Sharp had surrendered, we decided to return to General Fort. Our guides deserted us, for they decided to take the advice of the politicians and turn themselves in to the Japanese. Charlie Smith and I would have to fend for ourselves. Our return trip would take many more days, for we did not know the trails, and the rainy season was setting in.

An interesting phenomenon, the rainy season. Each day, after a relatively clear morning, it rained from mid-afternoon until after dark, making for miserable hiking and camping conditions.

Believing now that the Japanese were occupying all the towns and barrios, we decided to keep to the jungle, even though this would force us to make camp in the rain and find our own food. We abandoned this brilliant strategy after one day and night. We struggled to find enough dry wood under fallen trees to have a small campfire, and roasted a parrot that Smith had shot during the day. His shooting this bird caused a minor rift between us, for I was convinced that the noise of his rifle would draw a horde of Japanese soldiers to us. I forgave him for his indiscretion as I chewed the meat off a leg bone, for that was the only food we had that day. Hungry, wet, and tired, we decided to take our chances on the barrios, and hope for the best.

During this hike I opined that the best time to travel in the jungle was during a rainstorm. When the afternoon rains began, we tried to keep as dry as possible and dodge all the mud holes on the trail, but after we got soaked from head to foot we found that walking in the rain and muck was less taxing than hiking in the hot, humid sunshine. Except for the damned leeches! We came to ignore them, and let them gorge themselves with our blood.

Having given up the idea of sticking to the jungle, we walked into a small barrio near the end of the next day's trek. It was deserted.

We decided to stay there for a few days to rest, dry out, and try to recover from our leech bites and sores.

The barrio had not been abandoned in a hurry. There were no personal items in the houses. The gardens had been carefully stripped—we found only a few camotes in the ground. And save for two chickens that had eluded capture, all the livestock was gone. We shot the chickens, dug up the camotes, and found a papaya tree still bearing a few ripe fruit. There was so little food available that this would be a haven for only a short while.

On the evening of our second day there, two natives who chanced to be traveling through the area showed us a lily-type plant and said the root was very good to eat. After they left I gathered several of the tubers. I peeled one and ate it raw. *"Not bad tasting,"* I thought. Then I carried the rest back to the hut where Charlie was resting. I sliced off a piece and gave it to him. But before he tasted it, my mouth suddenly started to burn like it was afire, and my stomach began to develop cramps like those I'd heard come with childbirth. Within five minutes I was in sheer agony, retching and puking with complete abandon. I was sure I had eaten a deadly poisonous plant, and considered death to be the preferable alternative to my misery. However, after several hours the pain subsided and I felt normal. Some weeks later I described this episode to some Filipinos. I was told that the root, like many other edible roots in the jungles, are mildly, but painfully, poisonous unless they are well cooked. Even the universally used root of the casaba, which is dried, ground into flour, then used in baking a tasty bread, is very poisonous when eaten raw.

We were nearing Bubong when we met some Filipinos who told us that we would find the going easier if we went by way of Kapai rather than by the trail we had planned to follow. We were weary of arduous trails, so we decided to take this advice, even though it would mean camping once more in the jungle in the rain. One more soggy night was a small price to pay for an easier trek. We moved on, looking forward to the comforts of the Bubong camp.

Charlie Smith and I got to the Kapai River soon after 8:00 A.M. There we found a one-hundred-foot-wide, rather swift stream, knee to hip deep. We crossed the river and met some friendly Moros along the bank. They told us that Sultan Penjamin Malna ruled the valley and offered to take us to him. Their urgency told us we had best not refuse. We walked along a fairly good, semi-graveled road, south past a school and on to the Sultan's house—a distance of a mile or two.

His house was an unpretentious structure set about eight feet above ground on stout poles. It differed from others in the village only by its ornate decorations and its tin roof, the latter a rarity in this remote area. It was surrounded by several small buildings and a well-kept garden of two or three acres.

We climbed the bamboo ladder leading to the living quarters and there met the Sultan. He was a nice looking fellow, quite tall for a Filipino, twenty-one or twenty-two years old. Attired in colorful robes and wearing the turban of a Moro datu, he greeted us pleasantly in structured English. He said we were about fifteen miles from Bubong, and that General Fort was surrendering to the Japanese at two o'clock that afternoon. It was now about ten o'clock in the morning.

"I can give you some horses and if you move very fast you could probably get to Bubong in time to surrender with the general," he said.

Charlie Smith and I looked at each other, then he replied, "Oh, we're just entirely too tired to go all that distance. Maybe we had better forget about surrendering with the general." Which we did.

We asked Malna if he would allow us to stay in the Kapai Valley for the time being. He showed us to a place some two hundred yards from his house, along the one main road leading up the valley. It was a low shed—barely high enough for my six-foot frame—thirty feet wide and fifty feet long, with a thatched roof and exterior walls of palm fronds. One end of the building had a dirt floor, the other end had a low, raised wooden platform for a floor.

We moved into the building with our few belongings and set up housekeeping on the wooden platform, along with millions of mosquitoes. If we covered ourselves at night to fend off the mosquitoes it got so doggone hot we nearly suffocated. If not covered up we were almost eaten alive. I longed for Undet, the Igorot who had been with me on my first venture into the jungles of Masbate, who built a smoke fire under our sleeping platform to keep the mosquitoes away. And all night long, the Moros walked up and down the road, talking loudly and whistling so that we would not think someone was sneaking up on us. In spite of all, though, this was paradise compared with the recent weeks in the jungle.

This was home for the next two months. We had no trouble getting food, carried water in long bamboo tubes from a stream not more than two hundred yards away, and relaxed almost as if we were on vacation—except for the constant worry as to when the Japanese would move in.

I never delved into the relationship between the Mohammedan religion and the Hebrew religion, but neither accepts pork as an edible meat. Wild pigs got into the Moros' gardens quite often and the Moros would shoot them, and then would be reluctant to touch the carcass. They knew that we would eat pigs, so we would frequently have a Moro visitor who would say, "Sirs. I have killed a pig. Would you like it?" Of course, we never refused. The Moro would lead us to the dead animal, then insist that we carry it beyond the edge of his property before we gutted it and slung it on a pole to tote it home. We weren't skilled butchers, but we would hack off the hams and split the rib cage, then dine on fresh ham and barbecued pork ribs until the meat spoiled. Other parts we cut into thin slices that we hung on a clothesline to dry. But even jerked meat didn't do well in this climate, and we wound up throwing most of it away.

All in all, we ate quite well and rebuilt our strength and our resolve during those two months. We were able to augment our diet of rice and wild pig with *carabao* (water buffalo) milk, which has a much lower fat content than cow's milk. Occasionally we were able to negotiate a deal for a chicken, eggs, or bananas, all of which we fried in coconut oil. We also had quite a variety of vegetables, including camotes, corn, and plantain. Once in a while we got other vegetables that were strangers to us but were not bad to the taste. And for dessert we had bananas, pineapples, and a goodly supply of native chocolate molded in chunks in halves of coconut shells.

Our major shortage was cooking and eating utensils. We fried foods in a mess kit and boiled foods in my hard hat or pineapple juice cans over an open fire. Half coconut shells served as eating dishes and as mixing bowls if needed. And fingers were made before forks.

On our third day in our new home, a Japanese plane flew low over the area and dropped several dozen copies of the Manila *Tribune*, the major English language newspaper in the islands. The paper headlined the story of Japanese control over all of the Philippine Islands. This was not news to us. But the paper also said that the

Japanese had landed on the west coast of the United States at the mouth of the Columbia River at Astoria, Oregon, and were rapidly advancing toward Portland. The city would be under Japanese control in a few days, said one article. The paper also claimed that Los Angeles would be under Japanese control within a day or so, as their fleet was shelling the city from the Pacific. At the time we had no radios or other news sources and, while we doubted the newspaper stories, we did give some credence to the possibility that the United States was being occupied. This was very disturbing news, and it was weeks later that we heard an Allied news report by radio dispelling the rumor.

Soon after we were settled in the Kapai valley, several small groups of Americans straggled into town. They had escaped from a Japanese concentration camp in Dansalan, where they had been imprisoned when they surrendered. The first group to arrive told us that the Japanese had established a policy under which if anyone escaped, the American non-com in charge of his squad would be killed. If the escapee did not return, the next higher ranking American would be killed, and on up the line to General Fort, if necessary. We were soon able to verify that the Japanese had executed members of the command line up to and including Colonel Vesey, who had been my commander at Bubong, but that General Fort had been spared.

Soon other escapees came in, along with many Americans who had not surrendered—the evaders. Among those were Lowell "Bit" Holder, John Spruill, Nick Pociluyko, Bob Ball, Ben Farrens, Bill Johnson, and many others. Our thirty-foot by fifty-foot shed was quite crowded at times, but most of our visitors stayed only long enough to have a few good meals, then the "keep moving" bug would strike them and they would head farther into the jungle. All were wandering in search of—who knows what? They were ships without rudders, looking for a way to stay clear of the Japanese, to get back to the U.S. Army or Navy, and to eat in the meantime. They were no different from myself and the two Smiths, except that we had a plan—to sail to Australia when the wind was right, and we were merely biding our time until the north monsoon moved in.

Meanwhile, my sores from leech bites and from other miscellaneous cuts and bruises ulcerated. At one time, I had thirty tropical ulcers on my legs, from ankles to hips. Round and ranging in size from that of a dime to a silver dollar, each was a festering, weeping, rotten-skinned sore deep enough to expose the bone beneath. They were sickeningly odorous, yet not extremely painful. They worried me so much that at times I would talk to Charlie Smith about turning myself in to the Japanese to see if they could cure them. Charlie had several sores also, but not nearly as many as I had.

Being certain that this must be an affliction from which the natives also suffered, we went to the sultan and asked his advice. Did he have a medicine man who knew a cure? He told us to return the next day and he would have a man there to tell us how to treat them.

On our return we met a seventy-year-old Moro herb doctor. After he examined our sores, he said, "Tomorrow I will feex."

The next day he handed me a small bottle, containing twigs and leaves in a bath of oil. Then he took us into a nearby forest and showed us some bright red flowers. We were to pick these flowers daily, make a paste of them and apply it to all of our sores. Then we were to apply a hot, wet compress for half an hour, remove it, and rub the oil from the bottle on each sore.

The bottle of oil he had given me was very small, so I asked him how I could get more if we needed it. He said, "Oh. You need? Put coconut oil in. You shake. You use."

Whether it was the flowers or the oil or the hot pack that we applied I don't know, but our ulcers healed within two or three weeks.

We had heard tales about the Moros killing GI's for their guns. Concealing pistols and automatics was not a problem, but hiding a rifle was a bit more difficult. While I was fretting over my sores and doing not much else, I took to remodeling my .30-06 rifle. A .30-06 is about thirty-six inches long, with a wooden stock extending almost the full length under the twenty-four-inch-long barrel and breech mechanism. I cut the stock down to about two feet. When assembled, the barrel extended about a foot beyond the stock, but it made no difference in the operation of the piece. I could hide the unassembled barrel and stock in my bedroll.

Except in the towns where Japanese garrisons had been established, the occupation had little effect on the everyday life of the Filipinos.

And so it was that 4 July 1942 was celebrated in traditional style at Kapai. The center for the festivities was the schoolhouse, almost adjacent to our living quarters. Located on several acres of level ground, it was surrounded by a ten-foot-tall hedge of alternating clumps of hibiscus and gardenias, both in profuse bloom at the time. To locate the school, one had only to zero in on the source of the sweet smell of gardenias. Proudly waving on a pole at the school's entrance gateway was a gigantic American flag.

Americans and Moros from miles around had gathered to enjoy a day of drinking, singing, gambling (there was a cockpit set up in one area), dancing to a live band—but mostly eating. The center of the cafeteria-style serving table featured a gigantic leg of a bull that had been roasted over an open fire, complete with an array of sauces in halves of coconut shells to enhance the flavor of the beef. Nearby was a pile of barbecued beef ribs on a spread of banana leaves, with a different variety of sauces.

The table drawing the largest crowd held the appetizers. Deep-fried grasshoppers. Spread to cool on more banana leaves, the crisp little critters were picked up by the legs and eaten like shrimp. I screwed up enough courage to try a few and found them to be rather tasty. But I preferred the beef. I was told that in the markets, the female grasshoppers sell for about ten times as much as the males, being much more appetizing because of their eggs.

The formal entertainment consisted of instrumental soloists, mostly singing guitar players. There was one classical guitar player who was outstanding. Most appreciated by the Moros, however, was the interpretive dancing of an elderly Moro who graphically depicted an eagle who fell in love with a beautiful maiden and finally flew down and carried her home to his nest in the forest. It was a very impressive and detailed dance, polished by years of repetition.

Joramentado. A religious rite in which a Moro *swears* to do something, in this case kill a Christian. Doing so assures his entry into Heaven. All Americans were automatically considered to be Christians.

We began to hear stories of Americans losing their heads in encounters such as this. The sword used was of the kind borne by the woman who was out to avenge the death of her son when I was building roads, with Hassan as my assistant and guide, some months before. As strangers in a strange land, we grew increasingly uncomfortable with our position. We were a minority of two—no one knew or really cared where we were. We would never be missed. We became paranoid.

Not the least of those we feared was the man who had been our benefactor and provided a place for us to stay and food for our table—Sultan Penjamin Malna. We had noted seemingly irrational reactions by him on occasion, but we ignored these spates of anger over what we considered to be minor crises. Led by our growing fear of the Moros in general, we began to doubt whether Malna was quite as honest as we had believed, a thought that had been expressed by several of the Americans who had passed through Kapai. And we were getting the "keep moving" bug again.

Leaving would not be easy. We did not think that Malna would take kindly to our walking out on him. He had housed us, fed us, and had developed an almost daily routine of inviting us to his home for conversation over a few drinks of whatever alcoholic beverage he had available. He might consider our leaving a breach of social etiquette—or an insult to him—and the result could be fatal for us. We would have to plan and execute our departure diplomatically. Very diplomatically.

We were sitting with Sultan Malna on his veranda, sipping some local alcoholic beverage. He began to brag about a horse he had recently acquired—its fine conformation, its great speed. He took us into his house to a window overlooking a meadow where the horse was corralled. But the horse had broken through a fence and now was grazing in a garden that Malna prized. Malna shrieked, grabbed his rifle, and promptly shot and killed the horse. Charlie Smith and I later carried the dead horse to our home, butchered it, and feasted on it for a few days. However, the incident told us it was time to leave.

We discussed our plans to leave with Nick Pociluyko, the only other American in Kapai at the time. Nick was living with a Moro family and considered his living conditions there to be as good as he would find anywhere else at the time. He did not share our growing fear of Malna and declined to join us. But he did offer to cover for us if necessary. Meanwhile, Smith and I packed our gear, prepared to depart whenever the opportunity might come.

That chance came about a week later. Malna left town to visit a barrio several miles away for a day or so. After dark, Charlie and I shouldered our packs. Stepping outside and about fifty feet away from the building, we blasted our house with several bursts of rifle fire, creating a scenario of our being attacked and scared into running away. We ran to a little-used trail that led away from the town into the jungle and then hiked to the south. Somewhere in that direction was Deischer's camp—what or where it was we did not know—the destination of many of the Americans who had passed through Kapai. Once again, Smith and I found ourselves stumbling and sloshing through dense jungle.

I had suffered so much from tropical ulcers caused by leech bites that I took every preventive measure I could find to avoid them. One native told me to kill the leeches by dousing them with concentrated nicotine. On this advice, I steeped a handful of tobacco to as strong a concentration as I could make. With a pint whisky bottle of the brew in my hip pocket, I was prepared to do in the leeches before they did me in.

Sometime after daylight, while stepping over a fallen tree, I slipped, fell on my bottom, and broke the bottle of nicotine. I dumped the broken glass out of my pocket, but the juice had been soaked up by my pants. Soon my butt got to burning so badly that I had to pull my pants off. I found a stream, washed my pants, squatted, and gently sloshed the soothing water against my seared hide. But the damage had been done. I hiked the rest of the day naked from waist to shoes, with a blister on my butt as big as a small dinner plate, a sore that took two weeks or more to heal.

That night we came to a small barrio. A Moro, presumably the chief of the town, showed us half a dozen letters of recommendation from Americans that he had met over the last decade. Being illiterate, he had no idea of the contents of the letters, which, in general, said, "This crook of a Moro should not be trusted by anybody," an assessment which proved to be correct.

"You will guide us to Deischer's camp? No?" I asked.

"But, Sair, it is bery, bery far, Sair. It is many, many too far to go now. Mañana, Sair. You eat. You sleep, Sair. Mañana we will go." We spent the night in the Moro mosque.

After dark, the Moro sent a runner to Malna's home to ask whether we had his permission to leave Kapai, whether we should be guided to Deischer's, or whether Malna would like to have us killed. When the runner got there, Malna had not returned from his trip and the runner talked to Nick Pociluyko. Nick told him he felt sure that Malna knew we were leaving, that he believed we had Malna's permission, and he was certain that Malna would want us to be taken to Deischer's.

The next morning, soon after daylight, the Moro guided us to within a quarter of a mile of our objective. He pointed out the trail to the camp and left us.

At Deischer's camp we found fifteen or twenty Americans living under rather crowded conditions. We were accustomed to the good life we had enjoyed at Kapai, and stayed only two days before heading out toward a hacienda where two American civilians were reported to be living. One was the brother of Claude Fertig, who worked with us at Masbate Consolidated and later directed the army's engineering operations on Panay. The other was Charles Hedges, a lumberman.

A day's hike took us to the MacMichaels' hacienda near the town of Momungan. MacMichaels was an American veteran from the Teddy Roosevelt era who, after American imperialism was established in the Philippines at the turn of the century, took his army discharge in this land. He staked a claim in an area set aside for American veterans on Mindanao Island, married a Filipina who bore him four daughters, and established a fiefdom as he prospered as a farmer and businessman. There, we found Wendell Fertig, Hedges, and navy CPO Elwood Offret.

There, we also found clean, comfortable beds and close to gourmet meals. Daughter Helen, seventeen or eighteen years old and quite comely, had studied home economics at a school in Negros and had learned her lessons well. We five Americans spent much of our time as kitchen drudges: pounding dried bananas, rice, corn, and wheat into flour; grinding cocoa, coffee, and dried coconuts; pressing fresh coconuts to extract the oil for cooking. All this for two reasons: Helen set an excellent table—and being in her presence was sheer delight.

Soon after the Fourth of July, the Japanese had marched all the prisoners being held at Dansalan to Iligan. From there they were to be shipped to other camps. Along the road hundreds of American and

Filipino soldiers were shot or beaten and left dead or dying. This was the Bataan Death March in miniature. Fertig and MacMichaels had a collection of "dog tags" that they had taken from soldiers' bodies found along the Dansalan highway. They had no plans for them at the time, but would turn them over to the military authorities when the opportunity came.

We left after a week or so. The hacienda was about three miles east of the main highway—much too close for comfort, for the Japanese would certainly be occupying this artery shortly. We would be putting our hosts in peril if the Japanese should find us there—or even learn that we had stayed there.

Four of us moved westward, crossed the Argus River, and hiked through many miles of neglected banana groves to the coastal highway running between Iligan and Kolambugan. Offret remained behind, for he was suffering from a severe case of dysentery. He would catch up with us later. We chanced hiking on the highway, and we met many Filipinos along the way who assured us that there were no Japanese nearby at the time.

Five or six days later we arrived in Kolambugan, familiar territory to Charlie Hedges for he had been the superintendent of the lumber company there. The town is situated at the mouth of Panguil Bay, with the Province of Misamis on the opposite side of the bay. We moved into the convent, temporarily abandoned by the priests, for four or five relatively quiet days. Then the Japanese arrived—and we left.

We went only a few miles back into the hills, where a Filipino family took us in for the night. We had just begun breakfast—the usual *lugao,* boiled rice—when we heard shouts outside.

"The Hapons are coming! The Hapons are coming!"

Without finishing the meal, we grabbed our gear and ran—Smith and Fertig in one direction, and Hedges and I the other way. A run of only a few hundred yards took Hedges and me to the top of a hill from which we could see the house we had just left. It had not been a false alarm. We counted at least twelve Japanese soldiers milling around. We jogged along a trail that led down into a small valley and up the other side—and stopped short when we saw a Japanese soldier walking toward us. We turned onto another trail and ran like hell.

We slowed to a jog again after covering about a quarter of a mile, thinking we were in the clear. Suddenly two shots rang out. We knew they were intended for us when we heard the whine of the slugs passing over our heads. We ducked into the brush, crawled about two hundred feet to an almost vertical bluff about twenty feet high. We were in a little valley with a plateau above us. Overhanging the bluff was a tree with half of its roots exposed, somewhat like the roots of a mangrove tree except that the mangrove tree would have been in water. We crawled under the roots and lay there.

Soon we heard some Japanese talking near us. About twenty minutes later the voices were directly above us—Japanese talking to Filipinos—close enough to the vertical bluff that I feared they could hear our breathing. They left, and we heard nothing for several hours. We just lay there and sweated.

At about four o'clock that afternoon, we heard Japanese talking to children and could hear dogs. Hedges and I figured that the Japanese were hiring kids with their dogs to search for us. We didn't hear very much more, so we just lay quiet—and worried.

At sundown, we decided to move out under cover of darkness. We each had a revolver and a small bedroll—mine containing my modified .30-06 rifle. We stashed the bedrolls under the roots of the tree. We would have better mobility without those burdens. I crawled on all fours about two hundred feet to the northbound trail. I could see a fire burning at the trail junction, some one hundred feet away. Prudence told me to go about one hundred feet in the opposite direction, from where I motioned to Hedges to move up. Then he went up the trail two or three hundred feet and signaled for me to come ahead. Then it was my turn to move forward, and so we leapfrogged up the trail for some distance. When we thought it was safe, we took off. We walked this meandering trail for about half a mile as it followed a river. Then the trail crossed the river and we waded about chest deep across the one-hundred-foot-wide stream.

It was now about midnight. We came upon a native family's hut just across the river, perched eight feet above the ground on stilts, almost invisible among palm trees and banana plants. We woke the people by beating on the stilts and asked if they had seen any Americans pass there today.

The man said, "Oh yes, Sair! There are three Americanos very near here. I take you to them? Yes?"

Of course we said yes.

He came down the bamboo ladder from his hut and led us less than a mile to another dark Filipino hut. We beat on its stilts and soon heard voices—one clearly the voice of Charlie Smith.

"I'd know that voice anywhere," I shouted.

"Is that you, Ham? Holy hell!" he said. "We heard the Japs shootin' at you, and figured you were goners."

"Shit, Charlie," replied Hedges. "The bastards ain't got me yet, and if they do I'm takin' some o' them with me."

We crawled up the ladder and slept for a few hours—four Americans, a passel of Filipino kids and their parents, all bedded down on a ten by ten bamboo floor. It was rather cozy.

Charlie Smith had gotten directions to the home of a family by the name of Bolt to the south of us. After a predawn breakfast of boiled corn and rice coffee, we walked west a few miles to Baroy, where we picked up a partially paved road, and headed south. We did not know at that time if any Japanese were around or not, but took our chances. After a few miles we turned back to the east and found the Bolt evacuation place.

Mr. Bolt was an American who, like Mr. MacMichaels, was a Spanish-American war veteran who had stayed in the islands after serving out his enlistment in the service. He then had spent many years as a foreman at a cement plant in Cebu. After retiring, he moved to Baroy with his Filipina wife, where he built this very nice, very large house, a retirement home that now served well as a hideout from the Japanese.

Over the years Bolt had "gone native" and now blended into the native population—no longer distinguishable as an American. There were many Filipinos living with them, and families living in huts nearby—a cluster of abodes forming a self-sufficient community in the jungle. Some Americans had taken refuge there before us, only to stay for a few days and then move on, obsessed with the nomadic life.

I made a friend of one of the young Filipinos who offered to go back to the area where Hedges and I had hidden to try to find our gear. My directions must have been very accurate, for he returned a day later with all of our belongings.

While with the Bolts, I noted with much interest the importance of religion to these simple people—especially to the women. The bond of Catholicism among them was not lost on the enemy. The Japanese were not foolish enough to take extreme steps to try to eliminate the religion, but they made life difficult for the priests, and as a result some priests abandoned the convents and roamed among the barrios, conducting services wherever they happened to be on any day.

And so it was that a priest arrived at the Bolt compound to hear confessions and to say mass at the Bolt house. Mr. Bolt and we Americans—none of us Catholics nor, for that matter, practitioners of any religion at the time—sat on the porch while the devout of the area met with the priest for services inside the house. I was quite impressed by the effect of this ritual upon the practicing Catholics. That the tenseness and anxieties in almost all of them prior to the priest's ministrations had given way to serenity was immediately evident as they departed.

Morgan. Luis Morgan. William Morgan. Morgan Morgan. All of these names identified the same thieving, murdering, power-mad rogue who with his band of several hundred thugs roamed, raped, and plundered this portion of western Mindanao, under the guise of being guerrillas fighting against the Japanese invaders. His *army* had outstripped his control, and he asked Fertig to become the leader. Morgan would be "second banana."

Wendell Fertig considered himself to be a strong and intelligent commander. He doubted not his qualifications for generalship, although those skills were completely untested. Here was the opportunity to take command of an assemblage of misfits and convert them into a legitimate guerrilla organization and thus demonstrate his capability. He jumped at the chance.

Fertig asked Hedges, Charlie Smith, and me to take positions immediately below him in his table of organization. Hedges accepted, but Smith and I refused.

Charlie Smith and I, and to a large extent Chick Smith, our mechanical engineer co-worker at Masbate Consolidated (that seemed so long ago!), were still bent on sailing to Australia. We were fed up with the nomadic life—being the hares running before the hounds—and wanted to bid goodbye to the islands forever. Soon the weather would change, and with the northeast monsoon we would have the favorable winds needed for our journey.

"Have either of you ever done any sailing?" asked Fertig.

"No, Wendell, but I figure I'll learn on the way," replied Smith.

"And so will I, Wendell," I added. "And by darned, we'll make it."

Wendell pondered, then said, "I'm sure you fellows will learn to be sailors before I have learned how to be a general."

Charlie Smith and I had lost contact with Chick Smith. He was several years older than us, and tended to hide out rather than run away. We had heard that Chick was in Bonifacio and went off in search of him. If we were to set sail for the south, Chick, with his knowledge of things mechanical, would be an important member of our crew.

We hitched a ride on a fisherman's *banca* for part of the journey, moving at night through a rather swampy slough for about three miles to the open bay. Along this run, we passed under trees containing swarms of lightning bugs. In these tropical forests, they flashed simultaneously every fifteen seconds or so with a momentary brilliance sufficient to light up a newspaper for reading. After we crossed the bay, we sailed up a river until it became too shallow to float the boat. We waded ashore, then hiked warily toward the town, for we were unsure of the Japanese situation in Bonifacio, an unwarranted uncertainty, for the Japanese had been in town but left several days ago.

As usual when entering a strange town, we headed straight for the local convent. There we met Father Patrick Cronin, a twenty-nine-year-old priest born in Moneygall, Ireland. With customary priest's hospitality he invited us to breakfast, and offered us a place to sleep. Our immediate request was for information about Chick Smith. He told us that Chick, when the Japanese arrived a week ago, had moved about six miles into the jungle.

Father Cronin led us to him the next day. We found Chick living alone in a lean-to in the hills, surviving on food that Father Cronin or the natives living nearby brought to him. Chick, wasting no time in deciding, assembled his belongings in a few minutes and moved to town with us.

Father Cronin had not been harassed by the Japanese, for he was an Irish citizen and as such was a noncombatant. A Columban Father, he had been sent to the Philippines as a missionary only a few years earlier. He heard confessions on Saturdays and conducted mass on Sundays in a small chapel in Bonifacio. During the week he visited his parishioners in the outlying areas, traveling on horseback. Almost six feet tall, he made an interesting study in his white robe, astride a diminutive pony, his feet almost dragging along the ground.

"You must excuse me for offering you only tuba," Father Cronin said, as we sat around after an evening meal. "I would much prefer to serve wine to you, but I must save the few bottles I have for the sacraments. I know not where I will find more when my supply is exhausted."

We assured him that we considered tuba to be nectar of the gods, remembering our fear of the water we had drunk while plodding through the jungle.

"But, gentlemen," he continued, "I have a larger problem. My people say, 'Why do you allow the Americans to live with you in the convent, for they do not attend mass?'"

We told him that we were not Catholics—that, in fact, we didn't practice any religion—that we would not know what to do in a church service.

"But my people," he said, "they would be pleased if you attended, and my lot would be much easier."

Again we protested. "We would make fools of ourselves if we pretended to be Catholics."

"Not so," said the Father. "You need do only as the others do."

With this catechism we attended the services, knelt, made the sign of the cross, and stood when the others did—mimicked their every move. Father Cronin and the natives were pleased.

Many of our discussions in the evenings focused on our planned trip to Australia. It was now September, and we had a lot of preparations to make if we were to sail with the northeast monsoon. We asked Father Cronin if he would be interested in going with us. Although we were not of a religious bent, we believed that having a representative of the Almighty with us would certainly do no harm. He declined, citing his duty to continue to serve his parishioners.

"But you will need money to make your preparations," he said. "Perhaps I can help you."

We could not take an offer of money lightly, for that was the one commodity we most lacked. Yet we protested, or at least feigned it.

"Father, we appreciate your offer, but we will have to make do with what we have."

He persisted. "My parishioners feel the duty to contribute to the church. Many of the gifts are in the form of food or other items. But occasionally, coins and pesos are given to me. By church rules, I must accumulate these moneys and use them for the work of the diocese." He went on to explain that he had a considerable stash of cash which he was afraid might be stolen, or taken by the Japanese.

"It is money that belongs to the church. I must use it for a worthy cause, and I can think of no more worthy cause than to help you get to Australia."

We did not need a lot of convincing. He gave us three hundred pesos. We wanted to sign a note for this amount, so that the church could collect later.

"Oh, no," he said. "I won't take a note. I want to help you people get to Australia. If you don't get through, I would never ever think of asking your wives for this money. If you get there, pay me back. If you don't get there, I'll always feel that I did my best to help you people out."

In addition, Father Cronin gave us a Bible, along with his houseboy who wanted to go to Australia, too. I don't think that Father Cronin objected to our taking the houseboy, for he wasn't a gourmet cook.

We decided to hike to Pagadian, on the shore of Illana Bay, and there hire a boat to carry us to the Sarangani Islands. Sarangani, located off the extreme south tip of Mindanao, was a center known for its skilled fishermen and excellent boat builders. There we would seek out an adventurous soul with a good boat to take us to Australia.

From Bonifacio to Pagadian was a fifty-mile trek, for the trail wound its way through and around many mountains. Despite the condition of the trail, which was a washboard of ridges under six inches of mud—the trail was a main route for carabao caravans—and had many waist-deep streams to be crossed, we actually enjoyed the hike. We were rejuvenated. No longer were we plodding along without aim. We now had a definite plan. Admittedly some of the details were a bit hazy, but we could see light at the end of the tunnel—and that light was a sailboat to Australia.

eight

PREPARING TO SAIL

Our navigation chart was a *National Geographic* map covering the Pacific Ocean from the Hawaiian Islands to the Philippines, India to Australia. It was liberally peppered with pinpoint-sized dots indicating unnamed islands all the way from Mindanao to Australia.

The town of Labangan, about five miles northeast of Pagadian, proved to be a better place to stay for a while, for we were able to take up residence in a portion of a rice mill operated by a Chinese family. Our living area was a second floor loft normally used for storage of sacks of rice, but now empty. Our meals—typically Chinese fare of rice, fish, and strange vegetables—were "catered" by the Chinese family for a small fee. Although our quarters were dry and comfortable, the spilled grain in the cracks in the floor attracted rats that ran across us all night long.

For several consecutive days, we crossed the river and walked the five miles to Pagadian to buy supplies we thought we would need for our trip and to seek a boatman to take us to the Saranganis. We returned home each night without having made much progress on either score. We finally took an older native's advice to go farther south to the town of Dinapan. There, he said, we would find many seagoing Moros with boats for hire.

Leaving Chick Smith to guard our meager possessions, Charlie Smith and I hit the trail, and at Dinapan we had little trouble finding a boat and crew to take us to the Sarangani Islands. We inspected the craft—a sleek-looking *parao*—and with all the knowledge we land-lubbers possessed, pronounced it to be seaworthy. We arranged for the boat and crew to meet us at Labangan in four days. Charlie and I headed back afoot.

The crew arrived at Labangan on the appointed day, but with a much different boat—a *cumpit,* a cast off lifeboat from an inter-island steamer. It was no longer a rowboat. It now was wind-powered, with its oars replaced by a spindly bamboo mast and an oft-mended ramie cloth sail. It didn't appear to be very seaworthy, but we were deter-mined to get to the Sarganis, and since our route would be rela-tively close to shore for most of the way, we decided to chance it. Once there, we would find a better boat for our trip to Australia. After all, it was early in October, and we had two more months to make final preparations before favorable winds would be coming from the north.

Charlie Smith, Chick Smith, Father Cronin's houseboy, and I loaded our gear aboard and, with the crew of three Moros, set sail in mid-afternoon. About dark, the wind became quite strong, the seas changed from mild chop to roil, and our crew proved to be less-than-skilled mariners. The boat was not designed for tacking—we learned later that it didn't have a keel—and she rolled and pitched until all hands were seasick. By midnight, having made no progress against the wind and the heavy seas, we had no trouble convincing the Moros of the wisdom of returning to Labangan, for they were as scared as we were. Our only casualty was the loss of our houseboy, for he de-cided that life with Father Cronin was much more to his liking. He returned to Bonifacio.

Back at Labangan soon after dawn, we tried to get a refund of the down payment we had made before starting on the ill-fated jour-ney. This became a heated discussion, but when the Moros started to finger the hilts on their krisses, our demands suddenly softened. We negotiated a deal. They could keep the money if they would sell us the boat for a promissory note saying that we had commandeered it in the name of the United States Government and that the note would be redeemed when the Americans returned to control of the islands. Making deals like this had become a common practice between guer-rillas and civilians and, I'm sure, created a headache for the U.S.

Army Finance Department a few years later. With note in hand, the Moros walked home—and we now possessed a twenty-one-foot-long lifeboat with an eight-foot beam.

Chick Smith believed we could convert our new possession into a seaworthy vessel capable of transporting us fifteen hundred miles over the seas of Indonesia—and through the Japanese navy—to Darwin, Australia. Charlie Smith and I were convinced he was daft, although we agreed that a boat in hand was worth more than a boat we dreamed of.

We also agreed that we would begin our trip here in Labangan. No more trying to find a better jumping-off point.

With Chick Smith engaged in rebuilding our cumpit, Charlie Smith returned to Bonifasio and Misamis to gather supplies for our journey. Although Charlie now sided with Chick and leaned toward going with the cumpit as our craft, I was not convinced, and decided to seek out another boat, if one could be found.

On the day Charlie Smith left, Captain Morgan arrived in Labangan accompanied by a small band of his mercenaries. Although Wendell Fertig had taken command of Morgan's organization, he had not taken command of Morgan. The madman was like a loose cannon, and Fertig seemed to delight in Morgan's roaming at will far from Fertig's headquarters. Morgan had confiscated an eighty-foot-long steam launch belonging to a lumber company. Like our cumpit, it had been purchased with an IOU against the United States Government. He and his marauders were en route to the Zamboanga Peninsula on a raiding mission against the Japanese.

Being voluntarily in Morgan's company was as foolish as deliberately stepping into harm's way, but as I needed transportation to Malangas, where I hoped to find a better boat, I accepted his invitation to ride with him. En route to Malangas we stopped at every sizable village, where Morgan ordered a dance, a party, and the prettiest girl in town for the night. Ruthless, yet very personable, he had no difficulty getting the local citizenry to put on a celebration, and being a well-built, handsome man, he had no trouble attracting women. Morgan's men, too, found "sleeping partners" and this band, no doubt, left many pregnant young ladies in its wake. The partying converted what would have normally been a one-day sail, had we proceeded directly to Malangas, into a three or four-day event.

I found no boats suiting our needs at Malangas, but I was told there were trim sailing vessels to be had on Zamboanga Peninsula at Vitali, Morgan's next port of call. Morgan assured me we would be in Vitali in two days, and once there he would arrange for my return to Malangas in another two days while he proceeded down the peninsula in search of Japanese troops to harass. I could expect to be back with the Smiths in about a week. Instead, we sailed by day, partied by night—and arrived in Vitali ten days later.

In the company of a young man who had recently graduated from a forestry school, I conducted a fruitless search of the waterfront for a boat more suitable than our cumpit for a major sailing venture. I toyed with the idea of continuing the search in towns farther to the south, but when I realized that days were rapidly slipping by and the time of favorable northeast winds would soon be upon us, I decided to give up the search and head for home.

By that time Morgan had returned from his foray down the peninsula, where he had raided a town near Zamboanga City and destroyed its electric generation plant. Lacking any other method of transportation, I boarded Morgan's boat for the return trip to Malangas—a trip that took another week.

In Malangas I met a young Moro, Lakibul Nastail, a likeable chap who, on learning that I was planning to sail to Australia, expressed interest in going with me. He said he had access to a twenty-six-foot boat that he thought was very seaworthy. When I saw it, I agreed. With his brother and a friend, we sailed it to Labangan. I was shed of Morgan.

I had been on this jaunt for almost four weeks. Charlie and Chick were convinced that I had gotten into trouble and feared that I had been killed—by either the Japanese or the Moros, or by Morgan. It was a rather emotional homecoming, for the three of us were now bonded to each other like family.

Charlie had made his trip much faster than I, and had been pretty successful in finding some very important foodstuffs and other supplies. He had also picked up a husky Christian Filipino, Eugenio S. Catalina, a cargador who became his companion. Catalina, too, wanted to go to Australia with us.

With two boats to choose from, we now faced a difficult decision. My newly acquired boat was a typical native sailboat, long and narrow of beam and dependent upon outriggers for stability. Should we encounter a heavy storm, the outriggers could snap off and our journey would end at the bottom of the sea. The cumpit, being wider, could be made stable by adding a keel, thus eliminating the need for outriggers. And the cumpit would lend itself to being fitted with an engine and propeller, certainly important features in the event of calm seas, if we could find these items. After much vacillation, we decided to go with our first boat. Lakibul's opinion weighed heavily in this decision, for he obviously knew more than us about boats, sailing, and what we might expect when at sea.

We went to work on the cumpit. We added a four-inch by six-inch "sinker," a dense, heavier-than-water hardwood plank hewn from the trunk of a molave tree, extending the full length of the bottom. This weight would add the stability gained by a keel without materially increasing the draw we would need when sailing in shallow waters close to the islands we would be encountering. It would also protect the bottom of the boat if we chanced upon coral reefs. It would not help much in holding course when tacking, but we opted for shallow water maneuverability.

We replaced the bamboo mast with a stout mahogany tree trunk, stayed with very strong rattan vines, and found enough canvas to make a stronger sail. We should have replaced the bamboo boom as well, for in heavy winds we had difficulty holding it down. This proved to be a troublesome error in judgement.

We carried extra canvas, a few bamboo poles, and strands of rattan to repair masts and sails. While traveling, we rigged extra sails with canvas and poles wherever possible to pick up the wind.

Being a lifeboat, it had no hold, so we created one by adding a deck just below the top of the gunwales from bow to stern. This provided storage space to protect some of our supplies from the elements, but we still had no cabin space. Amidships we raised the decking about two feet higher to create a six-foot by eight-foot by four-foot high "cabin" into which we could crawl to get protection from the elements.

On Charlie Smith's recent supply-finding mission to Bonifacio and Misamis he had purchased two barrels of diesel oil and one barrel of gasoline. Why? Charlie answered, "I don't know. It seemed like a good idea at the time."

And it was, for he and I made several trips to the area near Pagadian and finally secured a shaft, a propeller, and a twelve-horse-power Japanese engine that ran on kerosene. We purchased this drive train with another U.S. Army IOU for one thousand pesos.

We mounted the engine high near the stern and angled the shaft through the transom well above the water line. Since the shaft was a bit too short, the two-foot-diameter propeller was only about half submerged. It was a Rube Goldberg arrangement, but it worked. We didn't have kerosene, but we experimented and found that a mixture of Charlie's "good idea at the time" gasoline and diesel oil worked pretty well.

We still needed storage tanks for fuel and water. In Pagadian, we found an abandoned life raft—a true raft on steel pontoons sixteen feet long and fifteen inches in diameter. It also had six odd-sized small flotation tanks. We converted the pontoons and the tanks into containers and were able to carry fifty gallons of gasoline, seventy-five gallons of diesel fuel, and a modest supply of drinking water that we planned to replenish as we traveled. We ran out of storage space and foolishly left twenty-five gallons of diesel fuel on the beach. Unfortunately, we had only about one half-gallon of engine oil,which became our most severe shortage.

Our food supplies were in sacks, boxes—any kind of containers we could find—stored wherever we could find space above or below deck. Our Chinese landlord and his wife made Chinese army field rations for us: fifty pounds of raw rice, deep-fried in coconut oil until quite hard and well cooked, then mortared and pestled into a powder. This and a sack of raw rice were our main items of food. We had ten pounds of powdered whole milk, twenty-five pounds of calamay, crude brown sugar, twelve cans of sardines, and several cans of very salty soybeans. A pile of coconuts stored on deck rounded out our food supply.

The galley was a two-foot-square piece of galvanized iron framed with angle irons, which we cantilevered off the port side of the stern. A bed of sand spread on it provided a place for an open fire for cooking. A grillwork of welding rods formed a seat for the pots or pans just above the fire.

Normally we would burn dried coconut husks to provide heat, but we carried a supply of hardwood kindling to use should we be lucky enough to have a fish or a piece of meat to broil.

Cantilevered off the starboard side of the stern was a similar-sized platform with a wooden bottom shaped much like a toilet seat, for that is what it was.

In addition to bolos, machetes, and pocketknives, our tools consisted of a pair of six-inch pliers, several open-end wrenches, a large screwdriver that showed all the signs of a previous life as a lever or as a chisel, a small screwdriver, a claw hammer, and a monkey wrench. The latter was an antique with a wooden handle and a square jaw—a "knuckle buster."

Our navigation chart was a *National Geographic* map covering the Pacific Ocean from the Hawaiian Islands to the Philippines, India to Australia. It was liberally peppered with pinpoint-sized dots indicating unnamed islands all the way from Mindanao to Australia. A child's pencil compass with a sharpened nail replacing the pencil served as dividers. Distances and compass bearings were determined with a celluloid combination ruler and protractor. To guide our steering, we had a Brunton compass, a mining transit about four inches square used in underground surveying.

Charlie Smith and I each had army issue .45-caliber automatics. I had my cut-down .30-06 rifle, Charlie had a Springfield rifle, Chick had a chromium-plated .25-caliber Spanish Star automatic. Our spare ammunition was minimal—not much more than could be carried in one hand. Lakibul and Catalina had knives and bolos. We were not a formidable, well-armed fighting force.

We considered our preparations complete at around noon on the fourth day of December 1942. It was "now or never" time. At four in the afternoon, Charles M. Smith, Athol Y. Smith, Moro Filipino Lakibul Nastail, Christian Filipino Eugenio S. Catalina, and I set sail from Labangan on the boat we christened the *Or Else*.

We would get to Australia—OR ELSE.

nine

TO AUSTRALIA

Before we left this *Shangri-la*, we made a trolling jig,
using some feathers from Charlie's birds. We "drug" that
lure from there to Australia—with nary a strike. That
probably sets a record for distance trolled without a bite.

With Charlie Smith at the helm, we headed southeast from Labangan
toward the Moro Gulf. It soon became evident that the molave plank
was a barely adequate substitute for a keel, for the *Or Else* tended to
heel over quite far, even if the wind was moderate. Chick and I busied
ourselves shifting cargo from place to place to give the boat better
balance. The adjusting of the load helped—but not much.

What little favorable breeze we had was soon lost, so we cranked
up the engine. Within a few hours it began to sputter. The sputtering
soon became a consumptive cough, followed by what might be termed
a merciful death. To conserve our fuel supply we had tested the engine for only a short time soon after it was installed and had decided
that an overhaul was not necessary. Having barely begun our journey,
we were still friends and we shared the blame for this lack of fore-
sight. Had this occurred two weeks later, we would have been at each
other's throats.

Chick Smith awaited daylight before dismantling the engine.
He tried a minor tuneup to no avail. After removing the head, the oil
pan, the piston, he pronounced his dismal diagnosis—followed by
his optimistic prognosis. The engine was so clogged with carbon,

gum, and miscellaneous goo that it needed a thorough cleaning. After a cleaning it would work fine.

Soon the parts of the engine were strewn across the deck and we all set to soaking and scraping. We spent our first full day at sea working without shade under an excruciatingly hot sun—so hot that when the sun set the mild night temperature felt uncomfortably chilly. It was noon of the next day when A.Y. poured our precious half-gallon of engine oil into the reassembled power plant and we heard the pleasant sound of the engine's chug and the splash of the half-submerged propeller as it churned us on our way.

We had been drifting with the current and the breeze—we had not lowered the sail—and were now out of sight of land. None of us had paid much attention to our location, but by consensus we decided that our destination, the Sarangani Islands, was to the southeast. A following wind allowed us to cut the engine as we headed in that direction.

I've heard of prisoners putting marks on their cell walls to keep track of the time spent in incarceration. Ours, too, quickly became endless days with each being the same as the one before. We didn't note the passage of time. We weren't sure if we had spent three days or four days covering the 250 miles to the Saranganis. Notches in the gunwales would have solved this problem.

Whether we had traveled three days or four days made no difference. We had barely made a dent in our supplies except for the lubricating oil, so we decided not to waste time landing at one of the Saranganis. Besides, we realized that at every island group along our route choosing an island to visit would be akin to playing Russian roulette. There would always be the risk of landing at an island populated by unfriendly natives or, worse, Japanese forces. The latter was a distinct possibility here since the Saranganis are located at the mouth of Davao Gulf, the access route to the Japanese stronghold at Davao City, Mindanao. We sailed along, well offshore, while we pondered our next course.

On the horizon some distance away and due south was an island. We guessed that it was Kawio Island, large enough to be named on our map. We headed directly toward that landmass, keeping it in sight over the bow all day. Darkness set in long before we arrived there, but as night fell we noticed a light on the island. The light now replaced the landmass as a target over the bow.

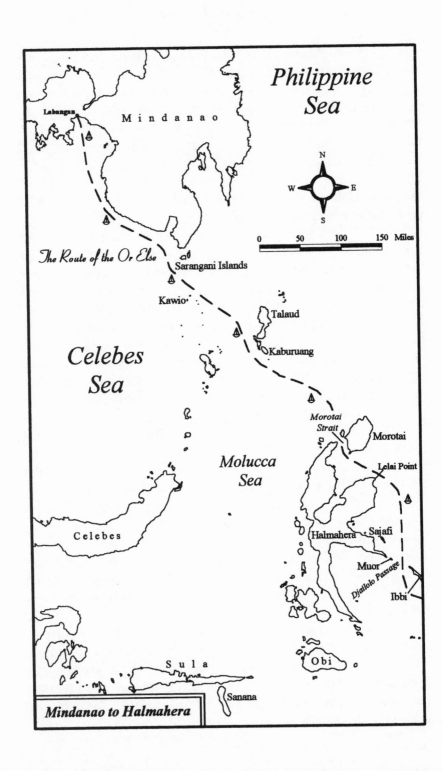

Philippine
Sea

Labangan
Mindanao

N
W · E
S

0   50   100   150   Miles

The Route of the Or Else
Sarangani Islands

Kawio

Talaud

Kaburuang

Celebes
Sea

Morotai
Strait
Morotai

Lelai Point

Molucca
Sea

Halmahera · Sajafi

Celebes

Muor
Djailolo Passage
Ibbi

Sula

Obi

Sanana

Mindanao to Halmahera

The following wind gradually shifted to port, and since our trusty craft did not make for successful tacking, we decided to lower the sail and proceed under power. Soon we were heading directly into the wind, and well after midnight we closed on the shore of the targeted land. We had been navigating by sight, ignoring the compass that was securely stowed in Charlie Smith's pocket. Now Charlie took the compass out of its leather case and discovered that we were moving on a *northerly* heading. Apparently, during this leg of our journey we had followed a circuitous route, drifting to the west and to the south. By aiming for a light instead of following a compass heading we had not compensated for the current and the wind. We had actually passed Kawio Island some distance to its west, and then approached it from the south. Our navigational skills needed considerable honing.

At dawn we moved close to the shore. We Americans were worried about having a language problem with the natives on the various islands as we proceeded to the south, a problem we had frequently struggled with while roaming around Mindanao. Lakibul assured us that he would not have a problem conversing here on Kawio, for he had encountered sailors from this island who carried on trade with the towns of southern Mindanao and he knew that there was much similarity in the dialects. Actually, we found as we traveled that the dialects on most of the islands on our route had enough Malay base to permit Lakibul and Catalina to make themselves understood.

Our Filipino crewmen held a shouting conversation with several natives casting large, round fishing nets along the shore. Assured that we were at a safe haven, we dropped anchor and they waded ashore to replenish our water supply. A leak had developed in the engine's cooling system and we had frequently refilled the radiator with our precious drinking water. This was a new problem which never was resolved and which made us touch land much more frequently than we wished.

Catalina and Lakibul also brought back some sun-dried meat, several gallons of coconut oil for fuel, and the welcome news that the Japanese visited Kawio from time to time but were not there at present. The Kawios also told them that a month or two earlier a boat had passed with several Americans on board. They had stayed one day and then headed south.

While Lakibul and Catalina were dealing with the Kawios, Charlie Smith and I dealt with our navigation problem. Chick Smith tinkered with the engine, all the while listening in on our conversation and adding his comments from time to time. We decided that for each leg of our journey southward we would start by determining where we were (ofttimes just a guess). Marking that spot on our *National Geographic* map, we would select the next island large enough to be more than a mere dot—hopefully one bearing a name—that was in the general direction of Australia. Then using the protractor to determine the bearing to that island, we would steer in that direction until we encountered land. If we decided this *was indeed* the island we were heading for, we would mark that spot and repeat the process. As it happened, with this system we sometimes changed course almost ninety degrees, both to correct navigational errors and to stay within sight of land on one side or the other.

To test our new navigational system, we selected Memanuke Island, about a mile long and a half-mile wide and only four miles from Kawio. As we were passing Memanuke and Charlie Smith and I were congratulating each other on our newfound skill, Catalina shouted, "Look there!"

We looked, and far in the distance to the right was what appeared to be a ship bearing down on us. This would be our first encounter with our greatest fear—the Japanese navy! Charlie quickly turned the boat toward the Memanuke shore and grounded it close to the beach. We jumped overboard and waded to shore.

We kept looking at the vessel, but soon realized that we couldn't detect any movement. We stared and stared—and eventually decided that any movement we were claiming to see was only a figment of our imaginations. Finally, we stuck two stakes in the ground aligned on the ship like gun sights. Still no movement. Near dusk we returned to the boat and shoved off, figuring that if it wasn't moving we could slip by under cover of darkness.

We were not more than five hundred yards off shore when we sighted a vessel that was definitely not a figment! It was a naval vessel, broadside to us at about five miles to the east on a course that crossed our beam. We turned, ran back to the island, and beached our boat again. We kept watching the cruiser—at least that is what we thought it was—as it kept going south and eventually disappeared from sight. It was two o'clock in the morning before we gathered the nerve to sail out again toward Kaburuang Island.

When dawn broke, we were able to identify the "ghost ship" we had seen the previous day. It was a small island with an extinguished lighthouse that together formed the silhouette of a very large ship.

As we sailed past it, Chick Smith said, "Fellas, if we hadn't panicked and dashed back to Memanuke we would have sailed right into the path of the cruiser."

"You're right, Chick," said Charlie. "I guess somebody up there likes us."

We passed Kaburuang well after dark, and by scaling the map distance I determined we had gone some 110 miles since leaving Kawio. We must have been sailing with a combination of very favorable winds, tides, and currents, for this calculated to be nearly six miles per hour—a speed our doughty vessel could ill attain. More likely, my calculations were inaccurate. No more accurate was my determination of the date, for this was either the tenth or the eleventh of December.

All through the next day and night and the following day we sailed southeast across the Molucca Sea toward Morotai. We had a good wind, and our clumsy boat heeled well over as we took advantage of a quartering wind. But it was hot as blazes throughout the day, and quite chilly by contrast at night. We were grateful for the few clouds overhead and spits of rain through which we passed, although they offered but fitful respite.

Mid-afternoon of the second day—or was it the third day?—on this leg of our journey, we passed through the Morotai Strait which separates Morotai Island from the north tip of Halmahera Island. After passing through the strait, we continued southeast with Lelai Point about ten miles to starboard. Through the night on what I guessed to be the twelfth of December, we sailed south past Sajafi Island toward the Djailolo Passage and Muor Island off the east coast of Halmahera.

As we approached Muor in the dawn we spotted a small power boat heading west. It ignored us, but we remained wary until it was well out of sight.

We arrived at Muor about 8:00 A.M. After a cautious approach, we anchored. Again we lucked upon friendly people. The arrival of an odd looking boat with even odder looking travelers brought the

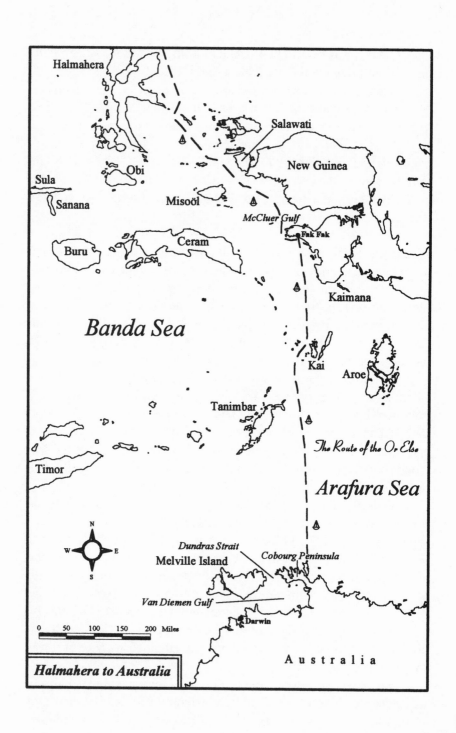

Halmahera

Salawati

New Guinea

Obi

Sula

Sanana

Misoöl

McCluer Gulf

Fak Fak

Buru

Ceram

Kaimana

Banda Sea

Kai

Aroe

Tanimbar

The Route of the Or Else

Timor

Arafura Sea

N
W ⊙ E
S

Dundras Strait

Melville Island

Cobourg Peninsula

Van Diemen Gulf

Darwin

0   50   100   150   200 Miles

A u s t r a l i a

Halmahera to Australia

native population out in force. We traded one of our makeshift pontoon drums—now empty of diesel fuel—for coconuts, vegetables, bananas, a fresh ham, and two chickens. We left Muor at about two in the afternoon, heading more or less east, with Ibbi Island on our port side.

We should have stayed at Muor for a couple of days to stretch our legs a bit. By generous estimate the *Or Else* had about 150 square feet of deck space. Stacked supplies occupied the front third of the deck, leaving about one hundred square feet to be shared by five men. It was impossible to move about the boat without bumping into or stepping on someone, and "excuse me" had given way to "get the hell out of the way." Lakibul and Catalina did not seem to be bothered, but arguments between the Americans came with more frequency each day and climaxed only four or five hours out of Muor. We argued about whose turn it was to take the helm, who should check the compass heading from time to time when one of the Filipinos was steering, who stank because he hadn't taken a thorough bath lately. With a critical shortage of matches, we argued about whose turn it was to tend the coconut oil lamp so we could restart the cooking fire and have a light for reading the compass at night. Charlie and I got into a hot argument about the lamp, and in exasperation he threw it at me! He missed, but managed to set fire to a pile of sail material, which we, fortunately, were able to extinguish before the boat went up in flames.

Around midnight I sat beside Lakibul at the tiller. We were in almost total darkness, and there was not a bump on the horizon to indicate the presence of an island. Charlie had gotten as far away from me as possible. He had cleared a space among the coconuts on the bow and had gone to sleep.

"Are we on course?" I asked. I wanted to check the heading, but the compass was in Charlie's pocket, and I wasn't about to wake him to get it.

"Oh, yes sair," said Lakibul.

"Are you sure?"

"I am sure, sair."

I was concerned about our course. But what difference did it make? We were moving. Going somewhere. And if we were going the wrong way, we could change course later. It wouldn't be the first time we went astray. Still, I was curious as to why Lakibul was so sure we were heading in the right direction.

"How can you be so sure without being able to see any islands ... or any stars?"

"I sail by the waves, sair."

"What are you talkin' about ... sail by the waves?"

"Sair, when you show me the way, I look at the waves. Then I go like this."

He demonstrated by using his one forearm to indicate the swell of a wave and his other forearm as the course of the boat, forming an angle with the wave.

"It is easy, sair, unless the wind moves."

When Charlie Smith read the heading with the compass in the morning, Lakibul was still within a few degrees of the course set the evening before, despite the fog we encountered in the early morning hours. I tried Lakibul's method on my next turn as helmsman and was off course by many degrees in a matter of minutes.

We realized that we needed a rest before tempers really flared, and decided to put in somewhere for a day or so. We were in the vicinity of Gag Island, but by preference we looked for and found an uninhabited island. We didn't need to confront any natives.

As Charlie Smith maneuvered our craft toward the shore of an unnamed island, Lakibul asked for a can of sardines to use for fish bait. We objected to wasting some of what we considered to be our emergency rations, but the prospect of a dinner of fresh fish made the idea worthwhile. We dropped the baited hooks overboard in water about thirty feet deep and immediately began catching three to four pounders similar to sea bass and red snapper. Charlie tossed the anchor overboard and joined in the fun. In the matter of an hour we had stringers of thirty or more fish.

Charlie maneuvered the *Or Else* to shore and we set up camp on the beach for the night. After exploring this small island next morning and assuring ourselves that it was uninhabited, and noting that it was beyond gunshot noise of any other islands, Charlie Smith shot a couple of birds. Catalina dug up some roots to cook for vegetables. Lakibul scaled a couple of coconut trees and gathered some young nuts.

That evening we sat down to a festive dinner of fresh coconut juice, fish, meat, and vegetables. What else could a man want?

Before we left this *Shangri-la*, we made a trolling jig, using some feathers from Charlie's birds. We "drug" that lure from there to Australia—with nary a strike. That probably sets a record for distance trolled without a bite.

We set sail early the next morning. Our short vacation on the uninhabited island had done wonders for morale. Although we didn't discuss this matter, we all realized that we had been pushing too hard to get to Australia as quickly as possible. We needed frequent stops—shore leaves, so to speak—and would have to risk going ashore frequently to keep from going stir crazy on this tiny craft, even if this delayed our arrival at a safe harbor on the Australian continent.

Again we sailed to the southeast. Our next major destination was the island of Salawati, off the northwest tip of New Guinea—a two or three day sail depending on the wind. When nightfall came we decided to anchor off the coast of a rather large island. We speculated on it being Fam, New Salai, Baialu, or Kailoof. Being so unsure of our location, we needed to await daylight to get our bearings.

It was a very beautiful night and we dropped anchor within one hundred feet of shore. A few hours after we got to sleep we were awakened by the sound of our boat scraping on the bottom of the sea. Apparently our anchor had slipped. We all jumped overboard and pushed the boat off the rocks, then reboarded and started the engine to continue on our way. We didn't seem to be moving as fast as we normally did when under power. At daylight we found out why. We hadn't stowed the anchor properly. It had fallen overboard and was dangling fifty feet below the boat in an ocean hundreds of feet deep. We had been chugging along under power with our brakes on.

New Guinea is shaped like a prehistoric bird when viewed on a map. It is the eastern anchor of the chain of islands forming Indonesia. According to our map, it was the halfway point of our journey to Australia. Salawati Island, separated from the main island by a very narrow pass, forms the beak of this bird at its northwest corner, and we watched the sun rise over this island on what I calculated to be 18 December 1942. New Guinea being the largest island between the Philippines and Australia, we reasoned that it was a most likely center of Japanese military activity. Prudence dictated that we proceed past Salawati to a smaller island. We chose Misool.

Five men, three of them having white skins, would certainly draw unwanted attention to the *Or Else.* The Smiths and I squeezed into the tiny cabin, leaving only the two Filipinos on deck to sail our craft into what appeared to be a small inlet. The sun, beating down on the roof of the cabin, made our hiding place an unbearable oven, and we soon crawled out and hid under pieces of sail material among the sacks of rice and raw coconuts.

A native in a baroto paddled up to our side. Lakibul, Catalina, and the native found enough common language to converse.

Soon Lakibul said, "Sairs, you can come. There are no 'Hapons.'" We welcomed his words.

We followed the native through a natural breakwater to a tiny bay with a small dock. We tied up and went ashore. Here we found a tidy little village with about fifty inhabitants. The houses were not on stilts like those we were used to seeing. They sat at ground level, connected by walkways paved with white, crushed seashells and edged with large stones. The village was set in a grove of small palm trees, and each house was landscaped with lush, flowering bushes.

Having strangers visit their island is a rare occasion for any native group, and calls for a celebration. We had no sooner docked the *Or Else* than the women began to prepare a feast. I knew we would be having chicken, for I could hear the birds protesting execution. Meanwhile, with Lakibul and Catalina as interpreters, we squatted with a group of men and inquired of the Japanese presence. They said that every week or two, Japanese soldiers visited villages along the south coast of Misool, but they had not yet come to this village, which was located on the western coast of the island.

After a good meal of chicken, fish, a meat which could have been dried beef but was more likely dog, rice, and camotes—all washed down with tuba—we began negotiations for food to take on board. While the women were very generous with the cooked meal, the men proved to be shrewd traders. A meager supply of vegetables, coconut oil, coconuts, fish, and smoked meat cost us a bolt of bright yellow cloth and most of our supply of tobacco leaves.

We left Misool at around four o'clock in the afternoon, well fed and content with the negotiations. About an hour later Charlie Smith said, "Hey, Ham. Where did you put the cigars?"

"I don't know where they are," I replied. "You had 'em yesterday."

Charlie and I had left Mindanao with a box of factory-made cigars, Manila's best, and had been smoking them sparingly to make them last throughout the trip.

"I can't find the damned things," Charlie said, as he rummaged through our gear.

Chick, who didn't smoke, said, "You might as well quit looking, Charlie. I swapped 'em for more food."

Within a few days Charlie and I were reduced to smoking dried coconut husk fibers wrapped in scraps of paper. It was like smoking corn silk behind the barn when we were kids.

We sailed to the southeast all night, and in the morning we neared McCleur Gulf. Viewed on a map or from the air, McCleur Gulf forms the huge mouth of the prehistoric bird, New Guinea. As we continued toward the southeast, we saw a large white yacht heading west from the gulf. Apparently it was under auxiliary power, for its white sails were fluttering. It looked out of place in this setting. It belonged in Newport, Rhode Island, or in San Diego, California—not in the Southwest Pacific. We considered contacting it, but not for long, and continued on our course.

We had moved closer to the New Guinea coast as we passed McCleur Gulf, for we intended to make landfall at Fakfak, on the peninsula forming the south shore of the gulf. This, we hoped, would be our jumping off point for the long haul across the Arafura Sea to Australia. Our route this far had been dotted with little, unnamed islands that afforded hiding places if we needed them. From here to Australia there was a dearth of little dots on the map. In addition, there was little doubt that the Japanese navy would be present along this route, for the Japanese were trying to find a way to land troops on the Australian continent, and the logical entrance was its north coast. We would soon be undertaking the most dangerous leg of our journey.

As we sailed across the mouth of the gulf, Charlie said, "Wouldn't it be funny if we sailed into Fakfak and found a lot of gentlemanly Dutch planters, sitting there enjoying their beer?"

"Yeah," I replied, "and then we'd go into a Dutch beer parlor and have a few while waiting for the ship that would take us to Australia."

Chick chimed in, "You guys better get outta the sun ... or stop smoking them coconut fibers."

Our conversation was interrupted by a very heavy current with high waves. Apparently we had met up with a tidal bore coming out of the bay, and the main wave was at least four to five feet high.

"Kee-rist!" exclaimed Charlie. "Where the hell did that come from?"

Nobody answered him, for we were busy diving to grab the stuff on the deck before it fell overboard.

The sea calmed rapidly after the big wave. We kept going, trying to reach Fakfak that night. When darkness fell, we had reached the Fakfak peninsula, but still had about ten miles to go to reach the town. We found a nice sheltered cove and anchored there for the night.

I awoke to hear Lakibul talking to a native in a small baroto. The little old man had spotted the *Or Else* when he set out from shore at dawn to check his fish traps.

"Meester Ham," said Lakibul, "this man, he lives at that place." He pointed to a shack about a half-mile down the shoreline. It would have been hard to spot had it not been for a small pier jutting out into the bay in front of the structure.

"Has he got water and food to sell us?" We needed to take on a full larder for this critical leg of our journey.

"He say he has, sair, and will give to us."

Lakibul and I climbed into the baroto and the native maneuvered his outrigger canoe toward the pier. Charlie and the others hoisted the anchor aboard and began to move the *Or Else* in the same direction. There was little wind, and eventually they started the engine. By that time our baroto had reached the pier.

We had taken to stashing our gun belts below deck, for we were certainly safe from a sneak attack out there in the vast ocean. I would usually keep mine at my side while sleeping, however. As we glided over the water in the baroto, I suddenly realized that I had left my .45 automatic and ammunition behind on the *Or Else*. I considered ordering the old man to return to the sailboat, but decided that Lakibul or I could certainly take him in a fight. There was no need to worry.

The shack we had seen was apparently the storage shed for his fishing gear. The old man pointed to a path leading to a large house farther from the shoreline. While he stayed at the end of the pier with his baroto, waiting for our sailboat to reach the pier, Lakibul and I walked about fifty yards on the path through tall palm trees towering above banana plants laden with fruit. Ripe coconuts, awaiting the eating, littered the ground. There certainly seemed to be an abundance of food here, and we should have no problem filling out our supply for our long journey to Australia.

The trail ended at the large wooden house. I was a bit surprised to see a house of hand-hewed and sawed lumber, for I had expected the usual bamboo and rattan construction. Here we were met by three Malays, probably the sons of the old man who supplied us with a water taxi moments ago. While they spoke a smattering of English, it was Lakibul's skill with several native dialects, abetted by sign language, that made conversation possible.

"Ask them how far it is to Fakfak," I said to Lakibul.

After many too many words and gestures for such a simple question, Lakibul said: "Sair, they say is twenty kilometers, maybe."

"Are there Japs there?" I asked.

Again there were many words and gestures, followed by, "Sair, they say are much Hapons in Fakfak. They say they come to this place many times. And maybe soon."

We discussed the food situation, and were told we could take anything we wanted from the ground and the trees. Hearing this, we thanked the Malays with many words and gestures, and headed for the pier to get help in gathering the food. Charlie Smith had anchored about two hundred yards off the nose of the pier, for the tide was out and he had to stay clear of the shallows.

As we began to cross the beach toward the pier I heard Charlie and Chick yelling, "RUN! RUN!"

I looked back toward the house. Coming pell-mell down the path after us were about a hundred natives, almost stark naked, faces streaked with war paint, carrying spears and shields, shrieking wildly.

Charlie grabbed his rifle and began shooting over our heads at the tribesmen, considerably slowing their pace. Meanwhile, A. Y. was cranking up the engine. Lakibul and I ran to the end of the pier. The old man was still there. We jumped into his boat, ordering him to take us out to the *Or Else*. He began to row toward the boat, but after he got out about one hundred feet the natives started to holler at him, and he turned and headed back toward shore.

"You dumb son of a bitch," I cursed myself. *"You carried that*

.45 on your hip for damned near a year, and now when you need it you don't have it."

I spotted a five-pronged fishing gaff in the boat, grabbed it and pressed it to the old man's belly. He got the message and turned again toward the *Or Else*. Meanwhile, the natives, yelling and screaming, ran back and forth along the beach. Some threw spears at us, which fell short, and some waded out toward us. When we got to our boat, Charlie and Chick had the anchor up and were ready to move out. And move out we did.

This had been our first serious encounter with any sort of enemy. I had no doubt that Charlie, Chick, and I would do anything necessary to protect each other and to complete our mission—escape to Australia. I had not had that kind of faith in Lakibul and Catalina, for we had known these natives for a very short time and I was unsure of what they might do if we ran into serious trouble. I remembered how the Filipinos had thrown down their arms and melted into the civilian population when the Japanese had taken over the Philippines. Would these two do the same when under fire?

Catalina and Lakibul must have sensed my fear about their loyalty. As Charlie, Chick, and I rehashed the attack, they sat apart from us—as apart as they could get on our tiny vessel—and after a long discussion in their native tongue, Lakibul said to us, "Sairs, not be afraid. We have be hungry, we have be thirsty many time. We will get to Australia. Not be afraid at all."

My question was answered.

After we had moved a mile or two toward the open sea, we looked back and saw a very long canoe with ten or fifteen men on board, making its way toward Fakfak. We felt sure they were going to contact the Japanese and tell them about us.

Now here we were. Counting every drop of diesel oil, gasoline, and coconut oil, we had about ten gallons of fuel. We had a limited amount of water, and an even more limited supply of food. We also had a dread of an encounter similar to that at our last stop if we went to Kaimana, the next island along the New Guinea coast. We decided to head straight for Australia, still more than five hundred miles to the south. Surely we would come upon another island—hopefully one populated by peace-loving natives and small enough to be of no interest to the Japanese—where we could replenish our supply of water and food. If not, we agreed, we would go on a starvation diet and subsist on the meager rations in our larder. The date was 23 December by my calculations.

Soon after setting a due south course, we encountered winds so strong we feared the boat might tip over. We all clung to the high side of the boat and kept full sails not only until dark but through most of the night. If the Japanese were looking for us, they probably would go to Kaimana, and we wanted to get as far from there as possible.

By morning, the pangs of hunger told us that a starvation diet for the next week was out of the question—that our supplies were insufficient for the rest of our journey. Even though a larger island would be a better place to find food, we were reluctant to put in at any such as Tanimbar or Aroe, lest it be occupied by the Japanese. But we were running out of choices. Land was getting harder to find.

Its size on the map made Kai Island a reasonable compromise. We resolved to chance a landing there. From Kai to Australia on a due south course would keep us equidistant from Tanimbar and Aroe. But that course also showed a paucity of tiny dots in a vast sea. If we couldn't get supplies at Kai, we were going to be in deep trouble.

We celebrated Christmas, my birthday, by opening our last two cans of fish. On the afternoon of the next day we arrived at Kai, which was surrounded by several smaller, barren islands—better described as sandy bumps on a large coral reef where a few hearty coconut trees managed to survive. We anchored the *Or Else* close to a beach for the night.

When morning came we were no longer close to a beach. We were *on the beach.* The tide was out and the beach had become several hundred yards wide. We were sitting in a tidal pool just deep enough to float our boat. This was not a problem as long as no one was attacking us, except that we had no water to drink, and could not find a source of that important fluid on the island. Lakibul climbed a couple of trees to harvest some coconuts. When he returned to earth, we breakfasted on coconut milk and soft, sweet, young coconut meat.

The boat floated free at about nine o'clock, and within an hour we were anchored near a village on the main island of Kai. There were many natives net fishing along the shore. We had only two five-gallon cans for water, for the bottoms had rusted out of the rest. Catalina and Lakibul took them into the village to fill them. We figured that it was best that we Americans didn't mix with the people, for we were certain that it was my white skin that drew the attack at New Guinea. They returned accompanied by three of the locals.

As many times before, through Lakibul's little knowledge of Malay, the natives' little English, and sign language, we learned that there were many Japanese at an air base about twenty miles to the east and that Japanese patrols visited this village several times a week.

We needed to get going fast, so we traded anything we had that was of value to the natives—even our spare pants and shirts—for food. We got some dried meat that was either pork or dog, two chickens, sweet potatoes, rice, corn, and native brown sugar.

Within a half-hour after leaving the village, two airplanes passed over us. They were climbing, so we assumed they were coming from the Kai airfield. We saw many large flights as we continued to the south on what became the longest leg of our journey—five days without sight of land. Although we were getting into the area where naval traffic could be expected, we did not encounter any large ships. I have no doubt that a periscope or two caught us in their views, although we didn't spot any breaking the surface.

On the second day out, we encountered small waterspouts, much like the "dust devils" seen on a desert. We maneuvered to avoid them for we didn't know how they would affect our tiny craft.

That night we were hit by a series of squalls that came from nowhere. We dropped the sail and rolled free on large waves. Charlie Smith and Catalina took shelter from the rain below deck in the tiny cabin, while Chick, Lakibul, and I were huddled under ponchos on deck, with Lakibul at the tiller. An especially strong squall hit us and the boat tipped over. The mast was flat out on the water. Chick, Lakibul and I were spilled overboard, along with all the supplies stored on deck. We clung to the high side of the boat, and as we clambered to get up out of the water, the boat righted itself. She was full of water, but stayed afloat. We bailed like mad for about an hour, using any container we could find that would hold water. We were cold, miserable, and scared.

The boat was finally emptied. The squalls departed, but not without taking a heavy toll. All of our water had been spilled. All of our rice, which we had been carefully rationing, had gotten wet. All of our sugar was wet. Save for a few floating coconuts that we were able to fish out of the sea, we were without water and had a minuscule amount of food. On the bright side, we still had a sail—and fuel for the engine. And best of all, we were still alive.

Near daybreak we encountered more rain. We quickly spread a large, black, rubber poncho and two small canvas tarpaulins on deck to collect water. We were so happy to be able to quench our thirsts that we drank the water from the tarpaulins as fast as we could scoop out a mouthful. When the rain stopped, we collected and saved a couple of canteenfuls from the poncho, only to find that it tasted so horrible as to be almost undrinkable—but we drank it. Fortunately, each night after sundown we encountered more rain and were able to drink some and save a few swallows for the next day. They were usually consumed before noon.

The next few days are the ones I'd like to forget. We jumped overboard frequently and clung to the side of the boat to escape the excruciatingly hot sun. Even in this there was no relief, for when we got back aboard the air temperature was at or above body temperature, and as it blew over our wet skins it made us feel even hotter. Between dips in the ocean, we took to huddling under our rain-collecting tarpaulins to hide from the sun and the wind.

When we could no longer stand the hunger cramps, we would hack open one of our precious coconuts, being very careful to share the juice and the meat with the others. If that was not sufficient food to satisfy the stomach, we would take a handful of wet rice grains, peel off the hulls, and pretend that the white morsels were delicious peanuts.

We kept scanning the horizon, looking for some semblance of land. Nothing. Could we, somehow or other, have missed the entire continent of Australia? At night we would look for lights—any kind of lights that would tell us we were not alone in the world.

During the day we steered according to the position of the sun, and at night by the stars. Charlie Smith or I would check the compass occasionally and make minor course corrections to insure that we were heading due south, especially when the stars were obscured by the clouds that brought our life-saving nighttime rain showers.

On the night of 30 December, Charlie was in the tiny cabin with Catalina and Chick and I were dozing on the deck while Lakibul was little more awake at the tiller.

"Hey, Ham," Charlie said. "You haven't checked the course for a long while."

"By God, Charlie, no I haven't."

I got up, struggled to read the compass by the light of the sky, and made a slight course correction. Then I looked up. I could see bumps on the horizon—that line where the blue of the sky met the deeper blue of the ocean. I squinted, not believing my eyes. There was land in front of us, to the right and to the left, blocking our path!

"Land! Land!" I shouted.

Immediately we were all on the deck, whooping it up loud enough for anyone within fifty miles to hear us.

"By God, Charlie, we made it!" Chick shouted, as he threw his arms about each of us in turn.

"Goddam! I knew we could do it!" Charlie yelled.

"Yippee! Yippee! Australia! Australia!" I cried, as I did a little dance.

Back at the tiller Lakibul and Catalina jabbered away, congratulating each other in Visayan.

As quickly as our celebration had begun, it ended. Everyone sighed—a sigh of relief. Each of us, in his own way, said a silent prayer of thanksgiving.

"Get closer to the shore," I said to Lakibul.

"But sair, we are now close. Too much close."

"No we're not," I said. "Move in closer."

Lakibul was right, for we were soon in very shallow water, where we anchored to await the daylight.

There was no doubt that we had reached Australia. But where were we? If we had held a true southerly course from Kai, we were probably, according to our map, on the coast of Arnhem Land. Assuming that to be correct, should we now go east—or west?

To the east was the Gulf of Carpenteria, a large body of water that could keep us at sea for several days trying to find a suitable place to land. None of the towns shown on the map around the Gulf of Carpenteria had names we recognized. To the west there was one town we had heard of before. Darwin. We decided to sail west.

By the light of dawn we examined the shoreline and saw the most inhospitable land we had encountered throughout our journey.

Sand dunes, and nothing else. We needed water, for we had had none for more than twenty-four hours. But there was no way that we could expect to find a stream spilling into the sea amid these hills. This land was completely barren—devoid of plant life and certainly devoid of animal life as well.

We sailed close to shore to the west for several hours, carefully studying the shoreline for any sign of moisture. We found none. Soon the land curved toward the north, and we had to lower the sail and move under power against the wind, using up our precious fuel. After an hour of motoring we rounded the point of a peninsula and were again able to take advantage of the wind.

Soon we noticed some scrubby plants on top of one of the dunes. In desperation we anchored, waded ashore, and climbed to the top of the dune, ready to tear the plants apart and suck the life out of their branches to get whatever moisture they contained. But that was not necessary, for immediately beyond the dune we saw a large, marshy lagoon.

Water!

We ran down the sandy slope and dunked our faces in the lagoon, gulping our fill before realizing that the lagoon was a stagnant lake. But stagnant, germ ridden, or whatever, we decided that with water at hand we would stick around and see if we could find some food.

Lakibul and I set out into a grove of eucalyptus trees to the south of the lagoon, armed with my cut-down rifle and his bolo. We must have walked about a mile before I spotted a couple of kangaroos within shooting distance. I have always considered myself a capable marksman, having brought down deer many times when hunting in the States. But deer only run in one direction—horizontally. These targets ran in two directions—horizontally and vertically. I shot at three of them and only encouraged them to move faster.

Lakibul and I walked back toward the boat, but having left no trail in the sand to follow, we hit the beach about a half-mile to the east of our destination. There, we saw a small shark trapped by the tide in a very shallow pool, feasting on tiny fish. I shot the shark, but only wounded it. Lakibul splashed into the pool and ran after the weakened creature, slashing at it with his bolo many times before delivering the telling blow. We returned to the boat, Lakibul carrying his three-foot-long quarry slung over his shoulder.

We had not outdone the two Smiths and Catalina. They had harvested a gallon of periwinkles, along with the heart of a palm tree. These, and pieces of shark, were soon boiling over a hearty fire, but not before we had consumed a goodly portion raw. We also boiled several gallons of the stagnant water and stored it aboard the *Or Else*. Safe and with bellies full, we all slept well as 1943 arrived. At least it was New Year's Eve according to my calculations.

New Year's Day found us sailing westward. We were making a gradual turn toward the south. Picturing our route for the last twenty-four hours and noting a large landmass to the starboard, we felt certain that we were rounding Cobourg Peninsula and entering the Dundras Strait between Cobourg and Melville Island. We were about to enter Van Dieman Gulf. Darwin was straight ahead.

It was almost sundown, and we were still holding a southerly course. To port we saw a large, very flat island, literally covered with birds of all sizes.

Chick Smith said, "Now, there's all the eggs we've wanted to eat for days. Let's spend the night there."

No one objected. We would go to the island, feast on eggs, and spend the night.

As we neared the island, darkness set in. In the tropics, there is no twilight. One can almost hear darkness dropping like a curtain. When we looked to the southeast we saw a bright blinking light. We all saw it. Had we all gotten delusional at the same time? It had to be a lighthouse. But a blinking navigation light in the middle of a war zone? That's crazy! We forgot about the little island and its promised egg feast and headed directly toward the light.

It was midnight before we came to the bluff occupied by the lighthouse, its light still blinking. There was little to do but await daylight. For some unknown reason, we were not too apprehensive about approaching this installation, despite not knowing whether the Allies still held Australia, or whether, like the Philippines, it had been invaded and overrun by the Japanese.

At about three o'clock in the morning, the tide ebbed and a bit of wind came up. The anchor dragged and the boat drifted toward the shore. Soon our keel was scraping and we wedged a couple of poles against the bottom to keep the boat off the rocks. When daylight finally came, we found the bluff to be a sheer cliff with no obvious way of scaling it. There had to be a way to get up there. We gambled that it was to the south.

We moved along the beach, trying to sail without the cooperation of the wind. Not feeling one hundred percent sure of our safety, we decided not to use the engine, so we poled the boat along, rounding a small point. The bluff gave way to a small beach with the lighthouse and some buildings several hundred feet above it. There were people walking on the beach and in the grove of trees beyond. We reasoned that there had to be a harbor nearby. But after we had sailed for about a mile, getting farther away from the lighthouse without finding a dock, we anchored and left Lakibul and Catalina on the boat, while the Smiths and I waded to shore through water about waist deep.

We walked back toward the lighthouse. The shore was rocky and walking was quite difficult. We heard noises in the brush along the beach, but we saw no one. Soon we came to a small opening in the bushes which seemed to be a path toward the lighthouse—blocked by five coal-black men armed with spears.

"Ye Gads!" I whispered to Charlie Smith. "This is just like Fakfak!"

Fortunately it wasn't. They were Australian aborigines who, we later learned, constituted a sort of home guard protecting the lighthouse. They spoke English well, and after they became convinced that we were not the enemy, they agreed to guide us to the lighthouse—albeit reluctantly.

They led us up an easy trail that switchbacked several times. About a hundred yards from the end of the trail, the natives called to the men in the lighthouse, then left us to continue on alone.

It was a sort of "Stanley and Livingstone" meeting—two Australians stuck off in a lonely wilderness greeting three Americans who appeared from out of nowhere. They led us into their large living quarters. All the while everyone was talking and no one was listening.

They soon realized that we might be hungry. One produced a couple of cans of meat and a can opener, while the other cooked up some sort of bread made in a skillet. A full-course dinner at the finest restaurant in San Francisco would not have been tastier.

We went into detail about who we were, where we had come from, and the horrors of life in the Philippines under the Japanese invaders. They were coast watchers and when they had seen us going by earlier they reported a *weird-looking boat* heading up the bay. We had seen a patrol plane responding to their call, flying low overhead as we were climbing the path to the lighthouse. When the same plane returned and circled over the area, one of the Australians radioed the pilot to call off the search.

We told them of our difficulty in finding a way to get to the lighthouse from the beach. They told us that during the night we had sailed past an entrance to a secluded harbor where their dock was located, and suggested that we move our boat there.

Chick Smith took a couple of cans of food for Lakibul and Catalina when he went to move the *Or Else*. The Australians, Charlie, and I made our way down another path to the dock. When the Aussies saw our "sturdy" craft, they marveled that sane grown men would trust their lives to an obviously inadequate vessel such as this. That we were willing to take that chance verified our description of the horrors of life in the close presence of the Japanese.

The Australians radioed information about us to Darwin—that three Americans and two Filipinos had sailed from the Philippines and were in need of fuel for their auxiliary engine so that they could continue their journey. The message was greeted with much skepticism, but finally the Australian navy said they would dispatch a vessel to assist us the next day.

What an evening! Two Australian coast watchers and lighthouse keepers in their late twenties and three American mining engineers-turned-sailors in their thirties and forties, comparing their nations, armies, navies, customs, mores, families, men, women, likes, dislikes, sports, travels, experiences, *ad nauseam* over several bottles of scotch, gin, and bourbon, while two Filipinos sat in the background stoically sharing the alcohol.

And woven into the conversation was the Australians' duty last night: an Australian convoy moving into Darwin needed the guidance of the Cobourg Light. It was the first night that the lighthouse had been illuminated for over a month.

Yes! Somebody up there really liked us!

The next day, as we were awaiting the rescue vessel to escort us to Darwin, we got to talking to our hosts about hunting and fishing.

"We sure could use a good boat for fishing," one of them said, gazing at the *Or Else*. "We've been looking for one for a long time, but ain't found one we like."

"I guess you guys really like your boat," the other Aussie said. "She must be a pretty good one to carry you fellows a couple thousand miles."

"That ugly little girl sure served us well," Charlie Smith replied.

"What are you gonna do with her, now that you're movin' south?" asked the other Aussie. "Put her in a museum?"

"I guess we'll give her to anybody that wants her."

"You wouldn't want to sell her to us, would you?"

I thought back to Masbate. When we left there, we had not much more than five dollars in our pockets. In this whole year we had survived with practically no money at all. Yet, we were going back to civilization. Would we need some pocket money? And if so, how much?

"Chick, Charlie," I said. "What's the *Or Else* worth to you?"

"Hell, Ham. She got us this far. She don't owe me nothin'," said Chick Smith.

"Likewise," said Charlie Smith.

"Okay, fellas," I said to the lighthouse keepers. "If we can ride to Darwin in the ship that's coming to help us, you can have her."

"For how much?"

"For free."

"No deal," said one of the Australians.

"Why?"

"'For nothing' would put a curse on her, and we wouldn't get no fish," said his buddy.

"That's only superstition," I said. "Take her."

"Nah. How about we give you a hundred quid for her?"

I had no idea what a quid was worth, but I sensed that a hundred of them was a lot more money than we had.

"It's a deal," I said, and we all shook hands to seal the contract. With a hundred quid in our pockets, Charlie, Chick, and I were rich men.

Rich and safe. What more could we ask?

ten

BRISBANE

Later, as the Smiths, the Filipinos, and I wolfed down plates of steaks and eggs, we agreed that today's flight, like every leg of our cruise in December, had been perfect. On all we had had a safe departure and a safe arrival. What occurred between was acceptable.

The next morning, 4 January 1943, we boarded an Australian navy corvette for the short ride to Darwin. She was returning to port after a tough battle against the Japanese in the vicinity of Timor, one of the Lesser Sunda Islands, where she had suffered considerable damage and lost several members of her crew.

After locating Timor Island on our navigation chart—our beat-up *National Geographic* map—I said to Charlie and Chick, "Look at this. We were almost within sight of each other a week ago."

"Yeah," said Charlie. "If they had spotted us then and picked us up, they sure would have made our journey much easier."

"Or they might have spotted us and blasted us out of the water," remarked Chick. "That would have made our journey to eternity much easier."

We docked at Darwin at four o'clock, exactly one month, almost to the hour, after our departure from Labangan, Mindanao.

At Darwin we were met by a high-ranking U.S. Air Corps officer and two military policemen who shielded us from the questions and the cameras of several Australian newsmen. We were immediately loaded into a staff car and taken to an airbase some twenty miles away. There we were quartered, fed, clothed—and confined. It was obvious that we presented the army with unexpected problems. I unintentionally added to them. While on our journey, my body had concealed outward signs of stress. Now the signs manifested themselves in the form of sores breaking out all over my body, accompanied by complete exhaustion and weakness. The medic who examined us ordered hospitalization for me. The Smiths and the Filipinos were given clean bills of health, and stayed at the airbase.

At the Australian army hospital in Darwin I was treated for salt-water boils, dehydration, and starvation. I was put on a seven-meals-a-day diet, and was given anything I wanted to eat as long as my selections were high in calories and proteins.

On the second day of my hospital stay, an Australian medical officer asked how I was feeling. I told him I was already beginning to feel great, adding that I couldn't remember ever having been fed so well before.

He asked, "Is there anything you want that you haven't been given?"

"Gosh," I said. "I can't think of anything—except maybe a bottle of beer or two."

"I'm not a beer drinker," he said, "but it's a good tonic."

He turned to the nurse and said, "Bring this man a quart of beer with every meal."

Seven quarts of beer a day is rather a lot. And beer isn't exactly something that goes well with cereal or ham and eggs. I drank a couple of bottles a day, and saved the rest for Charlie and Chick to enjoy when they came to visit.

But good times don't last forever. Mid-afternoon on a day about a week into my hospitalization, a doctor and several air corps officers arrived in a rush.

"Pack up your gear," they ordered. "You're leaving immediately."

"He can't leave now," said the nurse on duty. "I have hours of paperwork to do for his discharge."

"Use your imagination and fill in the forms without him," one of the officers suggested. Within a few minutes I was in a staff car en route to the airfield.

With Charlie, Chick, Catalina, and Lakibul, I enplaned in a Lockheed Lode-Star piloted by two Australian civilians.

"Where are we going?" I asked the copilot.

"I don't know about you, mate, but Mr. Carlson and me, we're going to Brisbane."

"How far is that?"

"Don't right know," he replied. "Depends on what towns they send us to on the way."

Mr. Carlson, the chief pilot added, "Right now we're going to Daly Waters. Shouldn't take us but an hour or so."

We were hardly airborne when we ran into a violent rainstorm. I was seated immediately behind the pilot's compartment, and could see through the open door. The plane's windshield was beating against the rain. Bolts of lightning flashed all around us. The plane was being bounced around severely, with Mr. Carlson fighting for control of the craft. Through the crackling noises of the radio the voice of a controller, safely on the earth below us, was giving him headings to follow.

I turned to Charlie Smith, seated across the aisle from me. "Charlie, I hope to hell these guys are better navigators than we were."

After an eternity that was probably no more than twenty minutes, we were out of the rain. Instead, we were darting from cloud bank to cloud bank and were rarely able to see the ground. From what I could hear of the radio voice and of the discussion between the pilots, I gathered that we were rather lost. I began to wish I was back on the *Or Else*, for I can swim but I can't fly.

More than an hour had elapsed since we took off. I could see a portion of the instrument panel and read a heading of 170 degrees on the compass, the same heading we had used immediately after leaving Darwin. *"We should be landing at Daly Waters any moment now,"* I told myself.

We finally cleared the cloud banks. Below us was a vast wasteland of sand. There may have been landmarks the pilots could identify, but all I saw was a tan blanket of nothing. We continued on for another half-hour, the radio still telling us we were on the right course.

Either a recognized landmark or dead reckoning told Mr. Carlson that we had passed Daly Waters. He made a 180-degree turn and we arrived over Daly Waters just after sundown. As we circled the field, someone in a jeep dashed along the runway lighting torches to mark its edges against the rapidly approaching darkness.

Later, as the Smiths, the Filipinos, and I wolfed down plates of steaks and eggs, we agreed that today's flight, like every leg of our cruise in December, had been perfect. On all we had had a safe departure and a safe arrival. What occurred between was acceptable. We also agreed that we would like our next move to be a little less eventful, but just as successful.

The following day took us to Brisbane, with one intermediate stop in Cloncurry, where the flies were more plentiful than were the swarms of mosquitoes in the swamps of Mindanao. Then on to Brisbane, where we were met by an equally thick swarm of U.S. Army brass, all eager to see "those characters who arrived from the Philippines." We were fed at an officer's club, then quartered in a hotel. In all the hubbub, none of officers realized that Catalina and Lakibul were nonwhites, and should not have been admitted to the club or the hotel.

In July 1942, General MacArthur created the Allied Intelligence Bureau (AIB) to carry out intelligence operations in the Southwest Pacific Area (SWPA). Composed of military intelligence groups from Australia, the Netherlands, England, and America, each carried out intelligence operations in the areas in which it had a national interest. Since America's national interest lay in the Philippine Islands, the American unit of the AIB was known as the Philippine Regional Section (PRS), under command of Col. Allison Ind. It was the PRS that had taken us under its wing at Darwin.

Colonel Ind wasted no time in subjecting us to interrogation. For more than a week we spent full days meeting with Ind and his assistants as they drew from us information concerning the conditions in the Philippines under Japanese rule, and about the budding guerrilla movement on Mindanao. Most of the interrogators had never been to the islands—had never, in fact, experienced warfare—for they had been called up for service after the war began and Australia had been their first overseas post. Throughout all the questioning, we tried to stress the importance of sending supplies to Mindanao to provide Fertig with the materiel needed to establish an effective guerrilla force.

"Colonel," Charlie Smith said, "with guns, ammunition, and

medicines, Fertig can run the Japs out of Mindanao. He's got plenty of troops, but nothing to fight with."

"You really think so, do you?"

"You're darned right I do. Fertig's got a whole bunch of Americans—navy, army, school teachers, priests, businessmen—who either avoided capture or escaped from Jap prisons. Good men, all of them, who realize that the only way they are ever going to get out of there is to win this damned war. They are now leading thousands of ill-equipped Filipinos who are just itching to get back at the Japs for what they have done to their people. Nobody would believe the way those yellow bastards are torturing and murdering the civilians for no reason at all."

Colonel Ind said nothing, waiting for Charlie to continue. Instead, I took over. "But the guerrillas' hands are tied, because they don't have anything to fight with but a few rifles, like one for every twenty men, and only a few rounds of ammunition for each rifle. They're fighting with bolos, spears, bows and arrows—anything to kill the bastards. They can run the son of a bitches out if they get the right tools."

Now it was Colonel Ind's turn. "I understand how you three feel," he said. "And I don't doubt that the guerrillas, given proper equipment, could wipe out every Japanese garrison on the island in a hurry. But, counting all the garrisons on Mindanao, how many Japanese troops are we talking about? A thousand? Two thousand? Five thousand?"

"A lot more than five thousand. Wouldn't you agree, Chick?" I said.

"Sure a lot more," replied Chick Smith. "More like ten thousand, I'd say."

"So," Ind continued, "we somehow send Fertig everything he needs to kill ten thousand Japs. What then?"

Recalling tales of Japanese atrocities, as told to me by people on the islands, I said, "Well, for one thing, there wouldn't be a bunch of Japs running around slicing off Filipino heads, raping women and young girls, killing babies. The people would be safe again."

"That's where your whole theory falls apart," said Ind. "The Japanese would pull a division of troops from some other front, move it to Mindanao, wipe out every guerrilla, and make the present mistreatment of civilians look like a joyful birthday party by comparison. Then they would send that division, minus the few casualties the guerrillas might manage to inflict, back to the major front to the south of the Philippines. It wouldn't take them more than a month to eliminate the guerrilla movement."

Charlie looked at me. Chick looked at Charlie. I looked at them both. The three of us suddenly realized that we had never seen the big picture. Nor had Fertig, nor all the other guerrilla leaders in the Islands. All we had seen was a little skirmish, a tiny part of a worldwide conflagration.

We paused to regroup, for we had come out of this conversation a poor second. Then Charlie Smith moved to another of our concerns.

"Colonel, when we left Wendell Fertig, we promised we would appeal for help for him and his troops if we were lucky enough to survive our trip. Well, we survived. Now we are asking for that help."

"Let me tell you this," said Ind. "You are not the first group of men to make it safely from the islands to Australia." This came to us as a mild surprise, although we certainly had no real reason to believe we were the first escapees.

"We interviewed one other group a week ago," Ind continued. "We also have sent several agents to other islands, who have returned with much information on the conditions in the Philippines. General MacArthur is aware of the suffering of the masses under Japanese rule. He recognizes that recapturing the Philippines is of paramount importance. He, too, has a promise to keep, for he has said to the Filipinos, 'I shall return.' But fulfillment of that promise is a long way off. The general has a plan to accomplish that goal. Guerrilla warfare on Mindanao is not of high priority in his plan at this time."

Until now I had been euphoric. Not only had we successfully sailed the *Or Else* to safety on the Allied side of the front, but we had had the opportunity to present the case for the Mindanao guerrilla movement to the army's top brass, a cause which we had considered all-important. Now I saw that we had failed miserably—failed to help the friends we had left behind in the islands. It was an empty feeling.

Charlie and Chick Smith and I sat licking our wounds over a few drinks at the Officer's Club bar before dinner. While we were not under house arrest or confinement, we were told it would be best if, for the time being, we mingled only with the two dozen or so AIB officers we had met. We were to restrict our activities to the AIB office, the Officer's Club, and the hotel, and should be careful to avoid contact with Australians and members of the press. Who we were and where we came from was "classified information," we were informed. Meanwhile, Lakibul and Catalina were confined at an army camp in the suburbs of Brisbane.

"What's next?" Charlie asked. "Where do we go from here?"

"I don't know about you fellas, but I'm getting out of here and back to the States as soon as possible," said Chick.

"Do you think they'll let us go back home? They seem to be hell-bent on keeping us under cover."

"Shucks. They can't keep us here forever. We're civilians, and civilians get repatriated."

"You sound like a jailhouse lawyer, Ham, but you're right. We got no ties or obligations to the U.S. Army, and they ain't got no hold on us. They sure as hell didn't help us get out of the islands."

That was the gist of our conversation throughout drinks and dinner. However, on meeting with Colonel Ind the next morning, that conversation became academic.

Ind looked at us in turn as he stirred his coffee. We were seated at the large conference table in a room adjacent to Colonel Ind's office, which by now had become familiar ground to us. It was here that we had been subjected to daily grillings.

"I think we've picked your brains bare by now. Right?"

"I guess so, Colonel," I ventured. "I can't think of anything else to tell you." Chick and Charlie murmured agreement.

"Good. Now all that remains is to send you home."

The three of us gave a boisterous round of applause.

"Man—excuse me, I mean *Colonel*—that sure is good news. When do we leave?" I said.

"Can't be too soon to suit me," said Chick.

"Can't be too soon to suit me, either," echoed Charlie.

"Well," continued Ind, "there is a problem."

"Please. Not a *big* problem."

"Actually, there are a couple of problems. First, we're not ready to let the public—and the Japanese—know that we have had direct contact with anyone from the Philippines. Of course, that news will leak out eventually, but we don't want the leak to come from you."

"Colonel, I *swear* I won't tell a soul nothin' about nothin'. And that goes for my buddies, too." They nodded agreement.

"I'm afraid that won't be good enough. It would be better if we kept you here for a couple of months. We could keep you away from prying eyes and ears."

My heart sank. "You mean, Sir, that we would be kept under wraps, like *imprisoned*, here in Australia for a couple months, to keep us from talking?"

"You can't do that to us," said Charlie. "We're civilians."

"Right," added Chick. "We must be repatriated. That's the law."

"Well, I suppose we could discuss the situation for a while and come to an agreement. But that could take a couple of months, too."

Charlie Smith slammed his hands down on the table. "Colonel," he shouted, "I'm a *civilian* and those birds on your collar don't mean a damned thing to me! You can't keep me here, and you don't have a prison that can hold me!" Chick and I added unprintable emphasis to Charlie's words, all three of us raging in unison.

After the noise subsided, the colonel raised his hand and, ignoring our protests, said very calmly, "Now let's get on with problem number two." At this point, I was duly confused. So were Chick and Charlie.

Colonel Ind went on. "You're right. You're not in the military, and I can't hold you here. If you want to go home, I can have you on a ship within a week.

"But ever since you arrived in Brisbane, you have been driving home the point that you wanted to get help for your friends who are stuck in the islands. Sailing home isn't going to help them at all."

The colonel stood and stepped up to a map of the Philippines hanging on a nearby wall. Facing it, he continued, "There is a way you can *really* help your friends, and play a big part in retaking the Philippines."

Ind paused again, then walked back and stood behind his chair. Very slowly, he said, "You can join the army."

We greeted this statement with hoots of forced laughter and guffaws. Almost in unison, we said, "Are you nuts?"

"Not really."

"Colonel," I said, "I've been there, and I know that I don't fit the picture. I'd just be another target for the Japs to shoot at."

"Ham's right, Colonel. I don't see myself as a guerrilla fighter, either," added Charlie Smith. "Besides, you said yesterday that General MacArthur isn't interested in guerrilla warfare just now."

Colonel Ind sat. "Your assessment of your fighting capabilities might be true, although I doubt it. However, while it is true that guerrilla fighting at present is of secondary importance, it is important as a harassment, to keep the Japanese off balance. But you can contribute much more in other ways.

"You men have firsthand knowledge of the islands: the terrain, the people, the enemy. You've proved that you know how to survive, both among the natives and in the jungle. All this is knowledge that makes you invaluable in preparing for our return to the Philippines— in laying the groundwork for a future massive military and naval assault. We need you, and others like you, to gather information, to build intelligence gathering networks, to establish lines of communication, and to open secure supply routes to the guerrillas.

"What I am asking you to do is certainly not without risk. Chances are you will be a much more important target to the Japanese in this role than you would be if you were a rifle-toting guerrilla. But you have demonstrated that you have the guts to do the job.

"If you sincerely want to keep your promises to the friends you left behind on Mindanao, the most effective way to do so is to put your knowledge to use. I can offer you direct commissions as captains in the U.S. Army if you will join the AIB team."

Colonel Ind rose. "Think it over, and let me know your decisions by tomorrow morning," he said as he turned to leave the room.

At the door he turned and added, "By the way. If you decide to return to your homes, you will be eligible for the draft. Are you interested in being buck privates?"

I sat there in stunned silence. Ind had asked us to put a reverse spin on our escape route from the islands. Instead of moving twelve thousand miles to the northeast from Australia to California, he wanted us to move two thousand miles back to the north.

Charlie Smith broke the silence. "What a salesman! He sure missed his calling."

"Yeah," said Chick. "How did you like the way our protests about being detained here rolled off him like water off a duck's back."

"You bet. So calm. So cool. He just moved right into the next step in his persuasion plan. He sure is a shrewd cookie."

"And how about the way he twisted our desire to go home? Made me feel like I was deserting Fertig and the rest of the guys in the islands. What a psychologist."

"Did you get how important we are to the war effort? How important all our knowledge of the geography and everything is? How about our 'guts'? What an ego builder."

"And then dangling carrots in front of the jackasses with the offer of commissions."

"Well I, for one, ain't buying it," said Chick. "I'm ten or more years older than you guys, and at fifty I'm too old to fight a war, unless they give me one of those soft-chaired desk jobs far from the front."

"Don't hold your breath. Those jobs are already filled."

"Let's go get a drink. I need one," said Charlie Smith.

"Me too, Charlie. We don't need to make up our minds until tomorrow morning."

Morning came, and Col. Allison Ind had scored a victory of two for three. Chick Smith, holding to his decision that he was too old for this game, requested repatriation. Charlie Smith and I signed up as captains, Corps of Engineers, Army of the United States (AUS).

By mid-afternoon—paper work completed—Charlie and I now had the right to roam the city without restriction—a minor benefit procured at disproportionately high cost. We walked without conversation toward our hotel, each deep in his own thoughts. Suddenly Charlie Smith broke the silence.

"Well, Ham," he said. *"Here we go again!"*

EPILOGUE

In May 1943, Capt. Jordan Hamner led a six-man team to Tawitawi Island, off the northeast coast of Borneo. As one of many AIB penetration parties inserted into the enemy-held islands in the South Pacific, his team's mission was to establish a coast-watching post and to report by radio to the AIB's station in Australia any ship movements spotted in the adjacent sea lanes. A second, but no less important, part of its mission was to gather and report general intelligence information in the Tawitawi-Borneo area.

The problem of maintaining his team's security in this area of intense Japanese presence required high mobility. Frequent moves from one vantage point to another were the norm—moves accomplished with great difficulty, considering the weight and bulk of the radio and its supporting gear and the terrain over which the moves were made. Frequently, the equipment was loaded onto a native sailboat and moved from cove to cove to stay one jump ahead of the enemy.

No less difficult was the problem of obtaining food, a task requiring frequent visits to native villages to purchase whatever was available. After a few months of inadequate diet and exposure to malaria-carrying mosquitoes, illness became a frequent problem. These problems, and a host of others associated with general well-being were solved and Hamner's mission was a success.

In early March of 1944, Captain Hamner returned to Australia by submarine. He was soon sent to the Pentagon in Washington, D.C., to present a firsthand account of the Philippine situation to its intelligence community. A month later he returned to Brisbane.

Captain Hamner then spent several months giving orientation lectures to army, navy, and air corps personnel destined to take part in the major assault on the Philippine Islands. Many of his lectures were given to naval and air corps airmen, telling them what they might expect should they be forced down among the natives.

Hamner participated in the Allied landing at Lingayen Gulf, Luzon, on 9 January 1945. Although he was not assigned to any particular combat unit, he moved south with the 11th Airborne Division and the 1st Cavalry Division, reaching Manila on 3 February. There he participated in freeing the Allied civilians who were imprisoned at Santo Tomas University. Many of these prisoners had been Ham's co-workers at the Masbate mines. All had endured horrible suffering during more than three years in the hands of their Japanese captors.

In March, a recurrent throat ailment caused Ham to seek treatment. He was transferred through a series of military hospitals for diagnosis and treatment. At Birmingham General Hospital, Van Nuys, California, a benign polyp was removed from a vocal cord. After a period of recuperation, Capt. Jordan A. Hamner was relieved from active duty. It was 18 March 1946. He soon returned to his profession as a mining engineer.

Hamner's Certificate of Service indicates that he received the usual decorations and citations awarded to all military personnel who participated in the various campaigns in the Pacific Theater. The certificate shows no medals recognizing the perilous nature of his contribution to the war effort.

Research indicates that Capt. Jordan A. Hamner was awarded the Legion of Merit medal on 2 October 1945 ". . . for exceptionally meritorious conduct in the performance of outstanding services. . . ." This was a very deserved accolade. It is unfortunate that no one in the United States Army bothered to tell Jordan A. Hamner.

Capt. Charles M. Smith moved north to Mindanao before Hamner set out for Tawitawi. Late in February of 1943, Smith and Lt. Cmdr. Charles Parsons, a naval intelligence officer, were sent as specially selected emissaries of General MacArthur to assess the growing guerrilla movement. Captain Smith had an additional assignment—to establish the first of many coast watcher stations. He set up the station on a mountaintop overlooking Davao Gulf to report Japanese shipping movements into and out of Davao City. This station remained in operation, manned by guerrillas from Col. Wendell Fertig's organization, without interruption throughout the war. One of its last transmissions reported a U.S. Navy task force moving toward Davao City in May 1945.

His assignment completed, Smith returned to Australia in late May of 1943. Smith was then sent to the United States to locate materiel suitable for clandestine missions in the jungles. The radio equipment and supporting gear he selected was shipped with highest priority to Brisbane, where it was repackaged in containers small enough to pass through the hatches of submarines. After an exhaustive search, Smith returned to Brisbane.

In early December of 1943, Captain Smith led a twelve-man party to the Philippines to establish a major radio network covering a large portion of the northern islands. His task was to provide coast watcher coverage of more than six hundred miles of major shipping lanes south of Manila, and to establish an intelligence gathering network covering Luzon from Manila south, and Samar and Leyte Islands—a geographic area of some ninety thousand square miles. Smith's party was augmented with a group of twenty-two men brought in by submarine in May 1944.

Soon after the Americans landed on Leyte Island in October 1944, Smith, who had now been elevated to the rank of lieutenant colonel, was transferred to 6th Army Headquarters. With that unit he participated in the Lingayen Gulf landings and the march to Manila, and met up with Hamner again in helping to free the prisoners at Santo Thomas University. Soon thereafter, Colonel Smith retired from the service and returned to his native Texas to become a gentleman farmer and cattle rancher.

Athol Y. "Chick" Smith was repatriated as he requested. There appears to be no record of his departure from Australia, nor of his destination stateside. He apparently faded into the civilian life he chose.

On learning that Hamner and Charlie Smith had joined the military, Eugenio S. Catalina and Lakibul P. Nastail hastened to enlist, and each returned to the islands with his respective American friend and benefactor. Only after Hamner and Smith left the islands after war's end did their faithful companions, Nastail and Catalina, return to their native homes.

APPENDIX

WAR DEPARTMENT
SERVICES OF SUPPLY
OFFICE OF THE PROVOST MARSHAL GENERAL
WASHINGTON

February 2, 1943

Mrs. J. A. Hazner,
　　c/o A. Dinwiddie,
　　　　Bishop, California

Dear Mrs. Hazner:

　　　　The Provost Marshal General directs me to inform
you that information has been received to the effect that
your husband, Jordan A. Hazner, an American civilian engineer,
has escaped from the Philippine Islands and has arrived
in Australia.

　　　　It is suggested that no publicity be given this
matter at this time.

　　　　Postal facilities between the United States and
Australia, while not normal, are still open and it is
assumed that Mr. Hazner will, if he has not already done so,
communicate with you.

　　　　　　　　　Sincerely yours,

　　　　　　　　　Howard F. Bresee,
　　　　　　　　　Lt. Col., C.M.P.,
　　　　　　　　　Chief, Information Branch.

The War Department notified Hamner's wife of his escape with
this letter, misspelling the last name as "Hazner."

FURTHER
READING

Chapman, James and Ethel. *Escape to the Hills*. Lancaster, PA: Jaques Cattell Press, 1947. An American educator and his wife lived in the jungle for more than a year before being captured by the Japanese.

Clausen, Henry C. and Bruce Lee. *Pearl Harbor: Final Judgement*. New York: Crown, 1992. Written by the independent prosecutor appointed by Secretary of War Henry L. Simpson in 1944 to investigate the causes of the Pearl Harbor disaster.

Disette, Edward and H. C. Adamson. *Guerrilla Submarines*. New York: Ballentine Books, 1972. Good account of the submarine activities in supplying guerrillas.

Dyess, William E. The Dyess Story. New York: G. Putnam's Sons, 1944. First story of an American's escape from a Japanese prison, published to inform the American public of the inhuman treatment being given the prisoners.

Earle, Dixon. *Bahála Na ... Come What May*. Berkeley, CA: Howell North, 1961. Relates the story of the ill-fated penetration of Mindoro by the Phillips party.

Fischer, Edward. *Mindanao Mission: Patrick Cronin's Forty Years in the Philippines*. New York: Seabury Press, 1978. Father Cronin tells of his life among the guerrillas.

Gause, Damon. *The War Journal of Damon "Rocky" Gause*. New York: Hyperion, 1999. Damon Gause and William Osborne escaped from Bataan and Corregidor, then made their way to Australia in a wooden boat, sailing some three thousand miles in fifty-two days.

Galang, Ricardo. *Secret Mission to the Philippines*. Manila: University Publishing Co., 1948. Account of a coast watcher's activities on Mindoro Island.

Gunnison, Royal Arch. *So Sorry, No Peace.* New York: Viking Press, 1944. Account of life as an internee at Santo Tomas written by a correspondent.

Haggerty, Edward. *Guerrilla Padre in Mindanao.* New York: Longmans, Green and Co., 1946. Memoir of a priest who secretly aided the guerrillas; describes day-to-day survival problems.

Harkins, Philip. *Blackburn's Headhunters.* New York: W. W. Norton, 1955. Account of one of the guerrilla units under Volckmann's command on Luzon.

Hunt, Ray C. and Bernard Norling. *Behind Japanese Lines.* Lexington, KY: The University Press of Kentucky, 1986. Good account of the Filipino aid given to Americans both in escaping from the Death March and in secreting them in jungle camps (Fassoth Camps) where they were given food and medical treatment.

Keats, John. *They Fought Alone.* Philadelphia: J. B. Lippincott, 1963. Highly fictionalized account based on Wendell W. Fertig's papers on the building of the Mindanao guerrilla organization.

Lapham, Robert and Bernard Norling. *Lapham's Raiders.* Lexington, KY: The University Press of Kentucky, 1996. Memoir of one of the multitude of guerrilla leaders operating in central Luzon during the Japanese occupation.

Lord, Walter. *Lonely Vigil: Coastwatchers of the Solomons.* New York: Viking Press, 1977. Good account of the activities of the Australian coast watchers who rescued John F. Kennedy and the crew of PT109.

McCoy, Melvyn H. and S. M. Mellnik. *Ten Escape from Tojo.* New York: Farrar and Rinehart, 1944. Account of the first escape from Davao Penal Colony written by the leaders of the escape. Members of this group were the first prisoners to be evacuated from the Philippines and returned to Allied control in Australia.

Rola, Ceferino R., 1st Lt., Inf., AUS. "Unit History of the First Reconnaissance Battalion Special." No Date. (National Archives). Unit history prepared in accordance with Army Regulations 345-105. Describes the staging camp and training for personnel of the penetration parties.

Schmidt, Larry S., Major, USMC. "American Involvement in the Filipino Resistance Movement on Mindanao During the Japanese Occupation, 1942-1945." Student thesis. U.S. Army War College, Fort Leavenworth, KA, 1982. Contains good annotated bibliography covering much of the activity of the guerrillas, including those beyond the subject island.

Spencer, Louise Reid. *Guerrilla Wife.* New York: Thomas Y. Crowell, 1945. Description of life for the Americans during the Japanese occupation. When the Japanese occupied Masbate the Spencers moved to Leyte, where Harold Spencer joined the guerrillas and Louise lived in the mountains.

Stahl, Bob. *You're No Good To Me Dead*. Annapolis, MD: Naval Institute Press, 1995. Details the activities of Maj. Charles M. Smith and his penetration party. This group landed on Mindanao 2 December 1943 and moved north to Samar soon thereafter to establish a large coast watcher network.

Tolley, Kemp. *Cruise of the Lanikai: Incitement to War.* Annapolis, MD: Naval Institute Press, 1973. Description of the cruise of a naval ship flying the American flag into Japanese territorial waters seeking to set up an "incident" between Japan and America.

Torio, Isaisas T., Cpl. and T/5 Albert Halla. "978th Signal Service Company." No Date. (National Archives). Unit history prepared in accordance with Army Regulations 345-105. Describes the training of radio operators and cryptographers who would become members of the penetration parties.

Travis, Ingram. *Rendezvous by Submarine. The Story of Charles Parsons and the Guerrilla-Soldiers of the Philippines.* Garden City: Doubleday, Doran and Co. 1945. Good account of Charles "Chick" Parsons' activities as General MacArthur's emissary in coordinating the guerrilla activities.

Volckmann, R. W. *We Remained: Three Years Behind the Enemy Lines in the Philippines.* New York: W. W. Norton, 1954. Relates his adventures in organizing one of the better guerrilla units on Luzon.

Willoughby, Charles Andrew. *The Guerrilla Resistance Movement in the Philippines: 1941-1945.* New York: Vantage Press, 1972. A collection of papers, documents and reports from the files of GHQ, U.S. Army Forces, Pacific. A good source of documentation, but poorly organized and difficult to use.

Wise, William. *Secret Mission to the Philippines: The Story of "Spyron" and the American-Filipino Guerrillas in World War II.* New York: E. P. Dutton, 1968. Details how Commander Parsons molded the multitude of guerrilla forces and mercenary groups throughout the islands into a useful military force.